We hope this book has been informative and helpful on your journey to understanding and celebrating older adults. Thank you for your interest and support!

Title: Political Landscapes: African Politics and Middle Eastern Dynamics
Subtitle: Navigating Diverse Political Realities and Socioeconomic Transformations

Series: Global Perspectives: Exploring World Politics
By Jonathan A. Sinclair

Table of Contents

Introduction

Significance of African and Middle Eastern Politics

African and Middle Eastern politics hold immense significance in shaping the global political landscape. These regions have a rich history, complex geopolitical dynamics, and diverse cultures that contribute to their unique political environments. Understanding the significance of African and Middle Eastern politics is crucial for comprehending global power dynamics, authoritarianism, and the state of human rights and civil liberties.

1. Historical Context and Colonial Legacies

To understand the present political realities in Africa and the Middle East, it is essential to delve into their historical contexts and colonial legacies. Both regions have experienced the impact of colonization, which has shaped their political structures, identities, and relationships with the rest of the world. The scramble for Africa and the partitioning of the Middle East by European powers left lasting impressions that continue to influence politics in these regions.

2. Economic, Social, and Cultural Diversity in the Regions

African and Middle Eastern politics are marked by remarkable economic, social, and cultural diversity. Africa encompasses a vast array of nations with diverse economies, ranging from resource-rich countries to those struggling with poverty and underdevelopment. Similarly, the Middle East comprises nations with varying degrees of economic prosperity, driven primarily by factors such as oil wealth and regional disparities. The cultural diversity within these regions further contributes to the complex political dynamics and power struggles that unfold.

3. Geopolitical Significance and Global Interests

Both Africa and the Middle East hold considerable geopolitical significance due to their strategic locations, natural resources, and economic potential. These regions are often caught in the crosshairs of competing global interests, resulting in interventions, alliances, and conflicts. The competition for resources, including oil, minerals, and strategic military bases, further amplifies the significance of African and Middle Eastern politics on the global stage.

4. Human Rights and Civil Liberties Challenges

African and Middle Eastern politics are also characterized by significant challenges concerning human rights and civil liberties. Many authoritarian regimes in these regions employ tactics to consolidate power and suppress dissent, often leading to violations of basic human rights. Understanding the complexities of these challenges, including the role of non-state actors, sectarian tensions, and the impact of regional rivalries, is crucial for addressing and promoting human rights in these regions.

5. Influence on Global Power Dynamics

The political dynamics in Africa and the Middle East have far-reaching implications for global power dynamics. These regions serve as battlegrounds for major geopolitical players, as well as arenas for cooperation and conflict resolution. The decisions made within these regions can impact global stability, trade, security, and the balance of power. Analyzing the significance of African and Middle Eastern politics provides insights into the broader patterns and trends that shape the world's political landscape.

In summary, the significance of African and Middle Eastern politics cannot be overstated. Their historical contexts, economic diversity, geopolitical importance, human rights challenges, and influence on global power dynamics all contribute to their importance in understanding the complexities of world politics. Through a comprehensive examination of these regions, we can gain valuable insights into authoritarianism, power dynamics, and the impact on human rights and civil liberties, ultimately contributing to a more informed and engaged global citizenry.

Historical Context and Colonial Legacies

To understand the current political landscapes of Africa and the Middle East, it is crucial to delve into their historical context and examine the lasting legacies of colonialism. The influence of colonization has left indelible imprints on the social, political, and economic structures of these regions, shaping their trajectories and contributing to the complexities we observe today. By exploring the historical context and colonial legacies, we can gain valuable insights into the root causes and historical factors that have shaped the political dynamics in Africa and the Middle East.

1. Pre-Colonial Africa and the Middle East

Before the arrival of European powers, Africa and the Middle East were home to vibrant civilizations and empires. These regions had diverse social, political, and economic systems that were deeply rooted in their cultural and historical contexts. Exploring the pre-colonial era provides a foundation for understanding the complexities and diversity that existed prior to external intervention.

2. Scramble for Africa: Colonization and Partitioning

The late 19th century witnessed the infamous "Scramble for Africa," during which European powers aggressively colonized the continent. Colonial rule brought with it various economic, political, and social transformations that significantly impacted African societies. European nations exploited Africa's resources, established colonial administrations, and imposed political structures that suited their interests.

Similarly, the Middle East experienced its own form of colonization, with the Ottoman Empire gradually weakening and European powers exerting their influence. The Sykes-Picot Agreement of 1916, in particular, played a significant role in redrawing the boundaries of the Middle East, contributing to the geopolitical complexities that persist today.

3. Colonial Legacies and Political Structures

The colonial period left lasting legacies in terms of political structures and institutions in both Africa and the Middle East. European powers imposed artificial borders that disregarded ethnic, tribal, and cultural divisions, leading to ethnic tensions and conflicts that persist to this day. Additionally, colonial administrations introduced governance systems that often favored European interests, which further exacerbated existing social and political divisions.

4. Nationalist Movements and Independence Struggles

The 20th century witnessed the rise of nationalist movements in Africa and the Middle East, as indigenous populations sought to reclaim their sovereignty and independence. These movements, fueled by a desire for self-determination and freedom, challenged colonial rule and paved the way for decolonization. The struggles and sacrifices of leaders and activists, such as Kwame Nkrumah in Ghana and Gamal Abdel Nasser in Egypt, played pivotal roles in shaping the post-colonial political landscapes.

5. Challenges of Post-Colonial Nation-Building

With independence came the challenges of nation-building. Newly formed nations in Africa and the Middle East had to navigate the complexities of forging a national identity, integrating diverse ethnic and religious groups, and establishing governance structures that could effectively address the needs and aspirations of their citizens. The legacies of colonialism, including resource extraction, economic dependence, and social divisions, posed significant obstacles to the post-colonial nations' progress and stability.

6. Continued Influence of Former Colonial Powers

The influence of former colonial powers remains palpable in contemporary African and Middle Eastern politics. Economic ties, geopolitical interests, and historical connections continue to shape the relationships between these regions and their former colonizers. The neocolonial dynamics and power imbalances have implications for issues such as foreign aid, trade agreements, and geopolitical alignments, underscoring the enduring impact of colonial legacies.

In summary, exploring the historical context and colonial legacies of Africa and the Middle East is vital for understanding the political landscapes of these regions. The Scramble for Africa, partitioning of the Middle East, and subsequent struggles for independence have shaped the complex dynamics we observe today. By examining the lasting effects of colonialism, we can gain a deeper understanding of the challenges and opportunities these regions face in their ongoing political journeys.

Economic, Social, and Cultural Diversity in the Regions

Africa and the Middle East are characterized by remarkable economic, social, and cultural diversity. The intricate tapestry of these regions reflects a multitude of experiences, perspectives, and challenges. Understanding the dynamics of economic development, social structures, and cultural variations is crucial for comprehending the complexities of African and Middle Eastern politics. In this section, we will explore the diverse dimensions of these regions and examine how they shape the political landscapes.

1. Economic Diversity

a. Resource-Rich Nations: Africa and the Middle East are home to countries endowed with abundant natural resources, including oil, gas, minerals, and agricultural products. These resources play a significant role in shaping the economic landscape and international relationships. Nations such as Nigeria, Saudi Arabia, Angola, and Algeria heavily rely on resource extraction for their economic growth and development.

b. Economic Disparities: Despite the presence of resource-rich countries, both Africa and the Middle East face significant economic disparities. Many nations struggle with poverty, unemployment, and underdevelopment. The challenges of wealth distribution, income inequality, and economic diversification pose substantial hurdles in these regions' economic progress.

c. Informal Economies: Informal economies play a significant role in the economic fabric of Africa and the Middle East. These informal sectors, comprising small-scale businesses, street vending, and subsistence agriculture, provide livelihoods for a substantial portion of the population. Understanding the dynamics of these informal economies is crucial for comprehending the socio-economic realities of the regions.

2. Social Structures and Identity

a. Ethnic and Tribal Diversity: Africa and the Middle East exhibit rich ethnic and tribal diversity, with numerous groups coexisting within each nation. The intricate web of ethnicities, languages, and cultural practices contributes to the social fabric and political dynamics. Examining the complexities of ethnic and tribal identities sheds light on power struggles, identity-based conflicts, and challenges in nation-building.

b. Religious Pluralism: Religion plays a significant role in shaping the social landscape of Africa and the Middle East. The regions are home to a diverse array of religious beliefs, including Islam, Christianity, Judaism, and indigenous faiths. The interactions and tensions between religious communities influence politics, societal norms, and cultural practices.

c. Gender Dynamics: Understanding the gender dynamics is crucial in assessing the socio-political landscape of these regions. Gender disparities, women's empowerment, and the role of women in political and social spheres vary across countries. Exploring the challenges and progress made in promoting gender equality provides insights into the diverse experiences of individuals within the regions.

3. Cultural Expressions and Traditions

a. Linguistic Diversity: Africa and the Middle East boast a wide range of languages, reflecting the cultural richness and diversity of these regions. From Arabic, Swahili, and Amharic to Berber, Hausa, and Yoruba, the linguistic diversity contributes to the uniqueness of each society. Languages serve as a vehicle for cultural expression, identity formation, and political mobilization.

b. Arts, Music, and Literature: African and Middle Eastern cultures are renowned for their vibrant artistic expressions, music traditions, and literary contributions. From ancient civilizations to contemporary art forms, exploring the cultural heritage and creative expressions provides insights into the values, aspirations, and narratives within these regions.

c. Traditional Practices and Customs: Traditional practices, rituals, and customs shape the social norms and identities within Africa and the Middle East. These practices often intersect with religion, gender roles, and community cohesion. Analyzing traditional customs provides a deeper understanding of the socio-cultural dynamics and the challenges faced in reconciling tradition with modernity.

In summary, the economic, social, and cultural diversity in Africa and the Middle East is central to understanding the complex political landscapes of these regions. From economic disparities and resource dependencies to ethnic diversity, religious pluralism, and cultural expressions, the diversity within these regions shapes power dynamics, social structures, and political interactions. By delving into these dimensions, we can gain a comprehensive understanding of the nuances and challenges that define African and Middle Eastern politics.

Chapter 1: African Political Landscapes Post-Colonialism and Nation-Building Challenges

The process of decolonization in Africa brought about newfound independence for numerous nations, marking the beginning of their journey towards nation-building. However, the post-colonial era was fraught with significant challenges that shaped the political landscapes of these countries. In this section, we will examine the impact of post-colonialism on Africa and delve into the various challenges encountered during the nation-building process.

1. Legacy of Colonial Rule:

a. Political Structures and Institutions: The legacy of colonial rule left an indelible mark on African political structures and institutions. European powers imposed centralized systems of governance that often marginalized traditional systems and concentrated power in the hands of a few. The challenge of reconciling these imposed structures with indigenous systems created tensions and power struggles.

b. Borders and Ethnic Divisions: The arbitrary drawing of borders during colonial rule disregarded ethnic, tribal, and cultural divisions, leading to enduring challenges. The post-colonial era witnessed ethnic tensions and conflicts arising from the artificial demarcations, as different groups vied for power and resources. Managing these divisions while fostering a sense of national unity proved to be a significant challenge.

2. Struggles of State-Building:

a. Nation-Building and Identity Formation: For newly independent African nations, the task of nation-building was complex and multifaceted. It involved forging a collective identity that transcended ethnic, linguistic, and regional divisions. The challenge was to create a shared national narrative while respecting diverse cultural traditions and aspirations.

b. Development and Modernization: Post-colonial African nations faced the challenge of addressing economic development and modernization. The transition from colonial economies, often focused on resource extraction, to sustainable and diversified economies required comprehensive planning and implementation. Balancing the needs of industrialization, social welfare, and economic empowerment posed significant challenges.

c. Governance and Institutional Capacity: Building strong institutions and effective governance systems was critical for stability and progress. However, many African nations struggled with corruption, nepotism, and weak institutional frameworks. The challenge lay in establishing transparent and accountable governance structures that could effectively address the needs and aspirations of the population.

3. External Interference and Neocolonialism:

a. Neocolonial Dynamics: Despite achieving independence, many African nations faced continued external interference in their political affairs. Economic dependencies, foreign aid conditionalities, and geopolitical pressures often undermined the sovereignty and self-determination of these nations. Understanding the neocolonial dynamics is crucial for comprehending the challenges faced in shaping their political landscapes.

b. Proxy Conflicts and Regional Instability: The Cold War era exacerbated political tensions in Africa, leading to proxy conflicts and regional instability. Superpowers supported rival factions, exacerbating internal conflicts and hindering the nation-building process. Managing these conflicts while forging a path towards stability and unity was a significant challenge for African nations.

4. Democratization and Political Reforms:

a. Democratization Waves: The late 20th century witnessed waves of democratization in Africa, as nations sought to establish inclusive and participatory political systems. The transition from authoritarian rule to democracy posed numerous challenges, including the establishment of democratic institutions, ensuring free and fair elections, and protecting human rights and civil liberties.

b. Role of Civil Society: Civil society organizations played a vital role in promoting democratic values, advocating for human rights, and holding governments accountable. The challenge lay in nurturing and empowering civil society to contribute effectively to the democratization process while navigating the complexities of state-society relations.

5. Case Studies of Successful Transitions:

a. Ghana's Path to Democracy: Ghana's successful transition from military rule to a stable democracy provides valuable insights into the challenges and opportunities encountered during the nation-building process. Examining Ghana's experiences sheds light on the significance of strong leadership, inclusive governance, and institutional reforms.

b. South Africa's Post-Apartheid Journey: South Africa's post-apartheid era presents a compelling case study of nation-building amidst the challenges of social divisions, reconciliation, and economic transformation. The country's Truth and Reconciliation Commission, efforts towards inclusive governance, and economic empowerment initiatives offer important lessons for other African nations.

Conclusion:

Post-colonial Africa faced formidable challenges in the process of nation-building, shaped by the legacy of colonial rule, struggles of state-building, external interference, and the pursuit of democratization. Understanding these challenges provides crucial insights into the complex political landscapes of African nations. By addressing these challenges and harnessing their diverse resources and potential, African countries can forge a path towards inclusive governance, sustainable development, and regional stability.

Ethnic Politics and Identity-Based Conflicts

Africa is a continent rich in ethnic diversity, with numerous ethnic groups coexisting within each nation. However, this diversity has also been a source of political complexities and identity-based conflicts. In this section, we will explore the role of ethnic politics and the challenges posed by identity-based conflicts in shaping the political landscapes of African nations.

1. Ethnic Diversity and Identity Formation:

a. Ethnic Groups and Cultural Pluralism: Africa is home to a vast array of ethnic groups, each with its own distinct language, customs, and traditions. Understanding the dynamics of these ethnic groups is crucial for comprehending the political landscape. Exploring the historical, cultural, and social dimensions of different ethnic groups provides insights into their aspirations, grievances, and political aspirations.

b. Identity Politics: Ethnic identities often play a central role in African politics, as individuals and groups mobilize along ethnic lines to pursue political objectives. Ethnic politics involves the use of ethnicity as a basis for political organization, representation, and resource allocation. Examining the dynamics of identity politics helps us understand power struggles, resource distribution, and the challenges of building inclusive political systems.

2. Historical Factors and Colonial Legacies:

a. Colonial Manipulation of Ethnic Divisions: During the colonial era, European powers often exploited existing ethnic divisions and hierarchies for their own administrative and control purposes. The imposition of indirect rule systems, favoritism towards certain ethnic groups, and the use of divide-and-rule tactics created enduring tensions and power imbalances. Understanding these colonial legacies is crucial for comprehending contemporary ethnic politics.

b. Ethnic Borders and Conflicts: The arbitrary drawing of borders during the colonial period disregarded existing ethnic, linguistic, and cultural divisions, leading to enduring conflicts. Border disputes, territorial claims, and struggles for self-determination have fueled ethnic conflicts in various regions of Africa. Examining these conflicts provides insights into the challenges of managing ethnic diversity and fostering peaceful coexistence.

3. Power Struggles and Resource Distribution:

a. Ethnicity and Access to Resources: Ethnic politics often revolves around access to resources, both economic and political. In many African nations, certain ethnic groups have historically held privileged positions in power and resource distribution, leading to marginalization and exclusion of other groups. Understanding the dynamics of resource distribution along ethnic lines is crucial for addressing the root causes of identity-based conflicts.

b. Competition for Political Representation: Ethnic politics manifests in the competition for political representation and influence. Different ethnic groups vie for political power and representation, seeking to protect their interests and secure a fair share of resources. Examining these power struggles provides insights into the challenges of building inclusive political systems that accommodate diverse ethnic aspirations.

4. Challenges of Nation-Building and Social Cohesion:

a. Nation-Building and Ethnic Fragmentation: The challenges of nation-building in Africa are closely intertwined with the complexities of managing ethnic diversity. Fostering a sense of national unity while respecting ethnic identities and aspirations is a delicate balancing act. Exploring the strategies employed by African nations to promote social cohesion and inclusive nation-building provides valuable insights into the complexities of political integration.

b. Grievances, Marginalization, and Identity-Based Conflicts: Identity-based conflicts often arise from deep-rooted grievances stemming from perceived marginalization, discrimination, or historical injustices. Examining these grievances and their manifestations helps us understand the triggers and dynamics of identity-based conflicts. It also underscores the importance of addressing historical injustices and promoting equitable and inclusive governance.

5. Peacebuilding and Conflict Resolution:

a. Mediation and Peace Processes: Ethnic conflicts require effective mediation and peacebuilding processes to achieve lasting resolutions. Case studies of successful peace processes, such as the ending of the Sudanese civil war or the reconciliation efforts in Rwanda, offer valuable lessons in conflict resolution and post-conflict reconciliation. Understanding these processes contributes to the promotion of sustainable peace and political stability.

b. Inclusive Governance and Power-Sharing: Inclusive governance models, such as power-sharing arrangements or consociational systems, have been employed in some African nations to address ethnic tensions and conflicts. Examining these governance models provides insights into the challenges and opportunities of building inclusive political systems that accommodate diverse ethnic aspirations.

Conclusion:

Ethnic politics and identity-based conflicts have shaped the political landscapes of African nations, presenting both challenges and opportunities for inclusive governance and nation-building. Understanding the complexities of ethnic diversity, historical legacies, power struggles, and resource distribution is crucial for addressing identity-based conflicts and fostering political stability. By promoting inclusive governance, equitable resource allocation, and addressing historical grievances, African nations can work towards building cohesive and inclusive societies that celebrate their diverse ethnic heritages.

Corruption and Governance Issues

Corruption and governance issues have long been significant challenges within the political landscapes of African nations. They undermine economic development, erode public trust, and impede efforts to build effective and accountable institutions. In this section, we will explore the complexities of corruption and governance issues in Africa, examining their causes, manifestations, and impacts on society and politics.

1. Understanding Corruption:

a. Definition and Forms of Corruption: Corruption encompasses a range of illicit practices, including bribery, embezzlement, nepotism, and abuse of power. Understanding the different forms of corruption provides insights into its mechanisms, prevalence, and impact on governance and public welfare.

b. Causes of Corruption: Corruption is influenced by various factors, including weak institutional frameworks, lack of transparency and accountability, poverty, and unequal distribution of resources. Examining the underlying causes of corruption helps us understand the systemic challenges that need to be addressed for effective governance.

2. Manifestations of Corruption in African Politics:

a. Grand Corruption: Grand corruption refers to high-level corruption involving political leaders, public officials, and business elites. It often involves embezzlement of public funds, misappropriation of resources, and abuse of power for personal gain. Exploring cases of grand corruption sheds light on the magnitude of the problem and its impact on national development.

b. Petty Corruption: Petty corruption, also known as everyday or bureaucratic corruption, occurs at lower levels of public administration and affects ordinary citizens. It involves small-scale bribery and extortion in interactions with public officials, such as obtaining permits, accessing public services, or avoiding fines. Examining petty corruption helps us understand its pervasive nature and its implications for governance and citizen-state relations.

3. Impacts of Corruption on Governance and Development:

a. Weakening of Institutions: Corruption erodes the integrity and effectiveness of public institutions, compromising their ability to deliver essential services, enforce the rule of law, and promote good governance. We will explore the challenges of building strong institutions and the impacts of corruption on their functionality.

b. Economic Consequences: Corruption hampers economic development by distorting markets, deterring foreign investment, and diverting public resources away from critical sectors such as health, education, and infrastructure. Examining the economic consequences of corruption provides insights into the challenges of achieving sustainable and inclusive development in African nations.

4. Socio-Political Effects:

a. Erosion of Public Trust: Corruption undermines public trust in government institutions, fostering a sense of disillusionment and cynicism among citizens. This erosion of trust weakens the social contract between the state and its people, hindering effective governance and citizen participation.

b. Social Inequality and Marginalization: Corruption exacerbates social inequality, as resources meant for public welfare are siphoned off by corrupt officials. This perpetuates poverty, marginalization, and unequal access to essential services. Exploring the social consequences of corruption sheds light on the challenges of promoting inclusive governance and social justice.

5. Anti-Corruption Efforts and Challenges:

a. Legal and Institutional Frameworks: African nations have implemented various legal and institutional mechanisms to combat corruption, such as anti-corruption agencies, legislation, and international conventions. Assessing the effectiveness of these frameworks helps us understand the challenges faced in combating corruption and strengthening governance.

b. Civil Society and Citizen Engagement: Civil society organizations and citizen-led movements play a vital role in raising awareness, advocating for transparency, and holding governments accountable. Examining the role of civil society in anti-corruption efforts provides insights into the importance of citizen engagement in promoting good governance.

c. Regional and International Cooperation: Regional and international cooperation is crucial in addressing corruption, as it often transcends national boundaries. We will explore initiatives, such as the African Union Convention on Preventing and Combating Corruption, and the role of international organizations in supporting anti-corruption efforts.

Conclusion:

Corruption and governance issues pose significant challenges to African nations, hindering their development, undermining public trust, and perpetuating social inequalities. Understanding the causes, manifestations, and impacts of corruption provides valuable insights into the complexities of governance in Africa. By strengthening institutions, promoting transparency and accountability, and engaging citizens in the fight against corruption, African nations can work towards building effective and inclusive governance systems that foster sustainable development and improve the lives of their people.

Economic Development and Foreign Aid Dependency

Economic development is a crucial aspect of African political landscapes, shaping governance, social dynamics, and international relations. Many African nations face significant challenges in achieving sustainable economic growth and reducing poverty. This section examines the complexities of economic development in Africa, including the role of foreign aid, resource management, and strategies for promoting inclusive and resilient economies.

1. Economic Challenges and Context:

a. Historical Context: Understanding the historical context of economic development in Africa provides insights into the legacies of colonialism, structural inequalities, and economic dependency. Exploring the impact of historical factors on contemporary economic challenges helps us comprehend the complexities of African political economies.

b. Structural Constraints: Structural constraints, such as limited infrastructure, inadequate access to finance, and low levels of human capital, present significant barriers to economic development in many African countries. Examining these constraints sheds light on the challenges faced in promoting sustainable and inclusive economic growth.

2. Foreign Aid and Development Assistance:

a. Role of Foreign Aid: Foreign aid has played a significant role in supporting economic development in Africa. We will explore the various forms of aid, including official development assistance (ODA), grants, loans, and technical cooperation. Examining the role of foreign aid helps us understand its impact on governance, dependency dynamics, and the challenges of achieving self-reliant economies.

b. Aid Dependency and Critiques: The dependence on foreign aid has generated debates and critiques regarding its effectiveness, conditionality, and long-term impact. We will explore the arguments for and against aid dependency, the potential distortions it creates, and the need for sustainable development strategies that go beyond aid reliance.

3. Resource Management and Economic Governance:

a. Natural Resource Wealth: Africa is rich in natural resources, including minerals, oil, and gas. However, the effective management of these resources and ensuring they contribute to inclusive economic development remain significant challenges. Examining the complexities of resource management sheds light on issues of transparency, governance, and equitable distribution of resource revenues.

b. Corruption and Rent-Seeking: The mismanagement of resources and rent-seeking behavior pose threats to economic development. We will explore the relationship between corruption, resource extraction, and governance, highlighting the importance of transparency, accountability, and effective institutions in resource-rich African nations.

4. Strategies for Economic Transformation:

a. Diversification and Industrialization: African nations are increasingly focused on diversifying their economies beyond commodity exports and promoting industrialization. We will explore the challenges and opportunities associated with economic diversification, including the development of manufacturing, technology, and service sectors.

b. Private Sector Development: The role of the private sector is crucial in driving economic growth and creating jobs. We will examine strategies for fostering a conducive business environment, attracting investment, and supporting entrepreneurship to stimulate economic development.

c. Human Capital Development: Investing in human capital, including education, healthcare, and skills development, is critical for sustainable economic development. We will explore the challenges and opportunities in human capital development, including the importance of addressing gender disparities and promoting inclusive education.

5. Regional Integration and Trade:

a. Regional Integration Initiatives: African countries have made efforts to enhance regional integration through initiatives such as the African Continental Free Trade Area (AfCFTA). We will examine the potential benefits of regional integration, including expanded markets, increased intra-African trade, and enhanced economic cooperation.

b. Challenges and Opportunities: Regional integration also presents challenges, including harmonizing trade policies, addressing infrastructure deficits, and managing diverse national interests. We will explore the opportunities and obstacles in realizing the full potential of regional integration for economic development.

Conclusion:

Economic development is a central aspect of African political landscapes, with significant implications for governance, social well-being, and international relations. By addressing the challenges of economic development, including foreign aid dependency, resource management, and strategies for inclusive growth, African nations can strive towards resilient, self-reliant economies that improve the livelihoods of their citizens. Fostering economic transformation, diversification, and regional integration are essential steps towards sustainable development and unlocking Africa's full potential.

Chapter 2: African Democratic Transitions
Democratization Waves and Political Reforms

Democratization has been a significant phenomenon in African political landscapes, with many countries undergoing transitions from authoritarian rule to democratic governance. This section explores the dynamics of democratization in Africa, including the waves of democratization, political reforms, challenges of building strong institutions, and the role of civil society in shaping democratic processes.

1. Waves of Democratization:

a. First Wave: The first wave of democratization in Africa occurred in the early post-independence period, with many countries transitioning from colonial rule to independence and adopting democratic systems. We will examine the factors that fueled this initial wave and the challenges faced in sustaining democratic governance.

b. Second Wave: The second wave of democratization took place in the 1990s and early 2000s, marked by the fall of authoritarian regimes and the adoption of multiparty systems. We will analyze the factors that triggered this wave, including global influences, regional dynamics, and internal pressures for political reforms.

c. Third Wave: The third wave of democratization witnessed further progress in consolidating democratic governance in Africa. We will explore the advancements made in electoral processes, human rights, and governance during this period, as well as the remaining challenges and setbacks.

2. Political Reforms and Democratization Processes:

a. Constitutional Reforms: Constitutional reforms play a critical role in shaping democratic transitions and establishing the foundations of democratic governance. We will examine the processes and challenges of constitutional reforms in African nations, including issues of inclusivity, decentralization, and protection of individual rights.

b. Electoral Reforms: Free and fair elections are central to democratic processes. We will explore the challenges and reforms aimed at enhancing electoral integrity, including voter registration, electoral systems, and the role of electoral management bodies in ensuring transparent and credible elections.

c. Judicial Reforms: An independent judiciary is essential for upholding the rule of law and protecting citizens' rights. We will examine the efforts to strengthen judicial systems, including judicial independence, access to justice, and the role of the judiciary in safeguarding democratic principles.

3. Challenges of Building Strong Institutions:

a. Executive Power and Checks and Balances: Balancing executive power and establishing effective checks and balances are crucial for democratic governance. We will analyze the challenges of creating institutional mechanisms that limit the concentration of power and promote accountability.

b. Legislative Reforms: The role of legislatures in democratic governance is vital. We will explore the challenges and opportunities in strengthening legislative institutions, promoting legislative oversight, and ensuring the representation of diverse interests.

c. Administrative Reforms: Efficient and accountable public administration is essential for effective governance. We will examine the challenges of administrative reforms, including combating corruption, enhancing transparency, and building capacity within public institutions.

4. Role of Civil Society in Democratization:

a. Civil Society Movements: Civil society organizations and social movements have played a crucial role in promoting democratic values, advocating for political reforms, and holding governments accountable. We will examine the impact of civil society in democratization processes, including their mobilization strategies, challenges, and achievements.

b. Media Freedom and Role: An independent media is instrumental in fostering democratic processes and ensuring transparency. We will explore the challenges and opportunities in promoting media freedom, access to information, and responsible journalism.

c. Social and Political Activism: Active citizen participation and engagement are vital for sustaining democratic transitions. We will analyze the role of social and political activism in shaping democratic processes, including youth movements, women's rights advocacy, and grassroots initiatives.

Conclusion:

Democratization waves and political reforms have transformed African political landscapes, offering opportunities for greater political participation, accountability, and respect for human rights. By implementing constitutional reforms, enhancing electoral systems, and strengthening institutions, African nations can continue on the path of democratic consolidation. The active involvement of civil society, media, and citizens is essential for sustaining democratic transitions and overcoming the challenges that arise.

Challenges of Building Strong Institutions

Building strong institutions is a critical aspect of successful democratic transitions in Africa. Strong institutions help establish the rule of law, promote accountability, and ensure effective governance. This section explores the challenges faced in building robust institutions in African nations, including the concentration of power, lack of checks and balances, corruption, and the need for capacity building.

1. Concentration of Power:

a. Executive Power: Concentration of power in the executive branch poses a significant challenge to building strong institutions. We will examine the consequences of executive dominance, including the erosion of checks and balances, limited separation of powers, and challenges to democratic governance.

b. Centralization vs. Decentralization: Striking a balance between centralization and decentralization is crucial for effective governance. We will explore the challenges associated with centralized governance structures, including the need for devolution of power, local autonomy, and strengthening local government institutions.

2. Rule of Law and Judicial Independence:

a. Legal Frameworks: The establishment of a robust legal framework is essential for upholding the rule of law. We will examine the challenges of creating comprehensive and enforceable legal frameworks, including issues of legal reform, harmonization, and ensuring access to justice for all citizens.

b. Judicial Independence: An independent judiciary is crucial for upholding the rule of law and ensuring checks on executive power. We will explore the challenges faced in ensuring judicial independence, including political interference, lack of resources, and the need for judicial reforms.

c. Access to Justice: Ensuring access to justice for all citizens is a fundamental aspect of strong institutions. We will examine the challenges of providing affordable and efficient legal services, enhancing legal awareness, and addressing barriers to justice, particularly for marginalized groups.

3. Accountability and Transparency:

a. Combating Corruption: Corruption poses a significant challenge to building strong institutions. We will explore the impact of corruption on governance, economic development, and public trust. Examining strategies to combat corruption, including anti-corruption laws, independent anti-corruption agencies, and transparency initiatives, will be crucial.

b. Financial Accountability: Ensuring financial accountability is vital for building strong institutions. We will examine the challenges associated with financial transparency, public procurement, and the role of audit institutions in holding governments accountable for public funds.

c. Freedom of Information: Access to information is a cornerstone of transparency and accountability. We will explore the challenges and opportunities in promoting freedom of information laws, strengthening the role of media and civil society organizations in accessing and disseminating information.

4. Capacity Building and Human Resources:

a. Institutional Capacity: Building institutional capacity is essential for the effective functioning of public institutions. We will examine the challenges of limited resources, skills gaps, and the need for training and development programs to enhance institutional capacity.

b. Public Service Reforms: Strengthening the public service is crucial for efficient and accountable governance. We will explore the challenges associated with public service reforms, including recruitment, merit-based appointments, performance management, and the need for professionalism and integrity.

c. Engaging Civil Society and Citizens: Building strong institutions requires the active engagement of civil society organizations and citizens. We will examine the challenges and opportunities in promoting citizen participation, civic education, and creating avenues for dialogue and collaboration between civil society and state institutions.

Conclusion:

Building strong institutions is a complex and ongoing process in African democratic transitions. Overcoming the challenges of power concentration, ensuring the rule of law, promoting accountability, and strengthening institutional capacity are crucial for sustainable democratic governance. By addressing these challenges and promoting inclusive and participatory approaches, African nations can lay the foundations for strong, accountable, and resilient institutions that uphold democratic values and serve the needs of their citizens.

Role of Civil Society in Democratization

Civil society plays a crucial role in promoting democratic values, advocating for political reforms, and holding governments accountable. This section explores the significant contributions of civil society in African democratic transitions, including their mobilization strategies, challenges faced, achievements, and their role in shaping democratic processes.

1. Definition and Importance of Civil Society:

a. Defining Civil Society: We will provide an overview of civil society and its role in democratic governance. Civil society encompasses a range of non-governmental organizations, community groups, and social movements that operate independently from the state. We will discuss the importance of civil society as a watchdog, advocate for social justice, and catalyst for democratic change.

b. The Benefits of Civil Society: We will highlight the benefits of a vibrant civil society in democratic transitions, including fostering social cohesion, promoting citizen engagement, providing a platform for marginalized voices, and offering alternative perspectives to state policies.

2. Mobilization Strategies and Advocacy:

a. Grassroots Movements: Grassroots movements have been instrumental in mobilizing citizens and advocating for political change. We will explore the strategies employed by grassroots movements, including community organizing, awareness campaigns, and peaceful protests.

b. Advocacy and Policy Influence: Civil society organizations have played a critical role in influencing policy-making processes and holding governments accountable. We will examine the strategies used by civil society organizations to advocate for policy reforms, including research, lobbying, coalition-building, and engaging with policymakers.

c. Media and Communication: Effective communication is key to mobilizing support and creating awareness of democratic issues. We will explore how civil society organizations utilize media platforms, social media, and other communication tools to disseminate information, raise public awareness, and foster public dialogue.

3. Challenges Faced by Civil Society:

a. Legal and Regulatory Constraints: Civil society organizations often face legal and regulatory challenges that hinder their activities. We will examine the barriers faced by civil society, including restrictive laws, limitations on freedom of assembly and association, and government interference.

b. Resource Constraints: Many civil society organizations operate with limited financial and human resources, which can affect their effectiveness and sustainability. We will explore the challenges of resource mobilization, fundraising, and building organizational capacity.

c. Repression and Threats: Civil society activists and organizations may face repression, harassment, and threats from state actors or non-state actors. We will examine the challenges posed by these threats and the strategies employed by civil society to overcome them.

4. Civil Society and Democratic Processes:

a. Election Monitoring and Observation: Civil society organizations often play a crucial role in monitoring elections and ensuring their credibility. We will explore the significance of election monitoring and observation, the challenges faced, and the impact of civil society's involvement on democratic processes.

b. Human Rights Advocacy: Civil society organizations are at the forefront of human rights advocacy, promoting and protecting civil liberties, and holding governments accountable for human rights violations. We will examine their role in promoting human rights, including issues of gender equality, freedom of expression, and minority rights.

c. Accountability and Transparency: Civil society organizations contribute to accountability and transparency in governance. We will explore their role in monitoring government performance, advocating for transparency in public institutions, and fostering citizen engagement in decision-making processes.

Conclusion:

Civil society organizations have played a significant role in African democratic transitions, advocating for political reforms, promoting citizen participation, and holding governments accountable. Despite the challenges they face, civil society organizations continue to be critical actors in shaping democratic processes, fostering social cohesion, and promoting inclusive governance. By supporting and empowering civil society, African nations can strengthen their democratic institutions and ensure that the voices of citizens are heard and respected.

Case Studies of Successful Democratic Transitions

Examining successful democratic transitions in Africa provides valuable insights into the factors and strategies that contribute to sustainable democratic governance. This section presents case studies of African countries that have experienced successful democratic transitions, highlighting the key drivers of change, challenges encountered, and lessons learned.

1. Case Study 1: South Africa

a. Historical Background: We will provide a brief overview of South Africa's history, including the apartheid era and the struggle for democracy.

b. Transition Process: We will explore the key events and processes that led to South Africa's successful democratic transition, such as negotiations, the role of Nelson Mandela and the African National Congress (ANC), and the Truth and Reconciliation Commission.

c. Key Success Factors: We will analyze the factors that contributed to South Africa's successful transition, including strong leadership, inclusivity, reconciliation efforts, and a commitment to human rights.

d. Challenges and Lessons Learned: We will discuss the challenges faced by South Africa during its transition, such as addressing socioeconomic inequalities, managing expectations, and navigating the complexities of post-apartheid governance. We will also highlight the lessons learned from South Africa's experience that can be applied to other democratic transitions.

2. Case Study 2: Ghana

a. Historical Background: We will provide an overview of Ghana's history, including its struggle for independence and subsequent democratic journey.

b. Transition Process: We will examine the key events and processes that led to Ghana's successful democratic transition, including the role of civil society, political parties, and the electoral system.

c. Key Success Factors: We will analyze the factors that contributed to Ghana's successful transition, such as a commitment to democratic principles, peaceful transfers of power, and a vibrant civil society.

d. Challenges and Lessons Learned: We will discuss the challenges faced by Ghana during its transition, such as corruption, economic development, and ensuring the sustainability of democratic institutions. We will highlight the lessons learned from Ghana's experience that can be applied to other democratic transitions.

3. Case Study 3: Senegal

a. Historical Background: We will provide a brief overview of Senegal's history, including its colonial past and post-independence political landscape.

b. Transition Process: We will explore the key events and processes that led to Senegal's successful democratic transition, including the role of civil society, the peaceful transfer of power, and the consolidation of democratic institutions.

c. Key Success Factors: We will analyze the factors that contributed to Senegal's successful transition, such as strong political leadership, a vibrant civil society, and a culture of democracy.

d. Challenges and Lessons Learned: We will discuss the challenges faced by Senegal during its transition, such as youth unemployment, regional inequalities, and maintaining political stability. We will highlight the lessons learned from Senegal's experience that can be applied to other democratic transitions.

4. Comparative Analysis and Common Themes:

a. Comparative Analysis: We will conduct a comparative analysis of the case studies, identifying common themes and factors that contributed to successful democratic transitions across the African countries.

b. Common Success Factors: We will identify common success factors, such as inclusive governance, respect for human rights, strong institutions, and citizen participation.

c. Challenges and Recommendations: We will discuss common challenges faced by these countries, such as corruption, socioeconomic inequalities, and the need for continued democratic consolidation. We will provide recommendations for addressing these challenges and ensuring the sustainability of democratic transitions.

Conclusion:

The case studies of South Africa, Ghana, and Senegal demonstrate that successful democratic transitions are possible in Africa. These countries have navigated complex challenges, built strong institutions, and fostered inclusive governance. By analyzing their experiences, we can gain valuable insights into the drivers of democratic change and the strategies necessary for building and sustaining democratic systems. These case studies serve as sources of inspiration and provide valuable lessons for other African nations embarking on their own democratic transitions.

Chapter 3: Middle Eastern Political Dynamics Historical and Geopolitical Factors Shaping the Region

Understanding the historical and geopolitical factors that have shaped the Middle East is crucial for comprehending the region's political dynamics. This section delves into the historical context and key geopolitical factors that have influenced the Middle East, including colonial legacies, regional rivalries, and the role of external powers.

1. Historical Background:

a. Ancient Civilizations and Empires: We will provide an overview of the rich history of the Middle East, highlighting the contributions of ancient civilizations such as Mesopotamia, Egypt, and Persia, and their legacies in shaping the region.

b. Islamic Civilization and the Caliphates: We will examine the rise and spread of Islam and the establishment of powerful Islamic caliphates that had a profound impact on the region's political, social, and cultural development.

c. Colonialism and Imperialism: We will explore the era of European colonialism and imperialism in the Middle East, including the Sykes-Picot Agreement, the mandates system, and the legacy of colonial rule on state borders, political structures, and identity formation.

2. The Arab-Israeli Conflict:

a. Historical Background: We will provide a comprehensive historical overview of the Arab-Israeli conflict, starting from the early Zionist movement, the Balfour Declaration, and the establishment of the State of Israel.

b. Key Events and Conflicts: We will examine significant events and conflicts that have shaped the Arab-Israeli conflict, such as the 1948 Arab-Israeli War, the Six-Day War, the Yom Kippur War, and the peace agreements between Israel and Egypt and Jordan.

c. Implications and Regional Dynamics: We will analyze the implications of the Arab-Israeli conflict on the region, including the rise of Palestinian nationalism, the role of non-state actors, and the impact on regional stability and security.

3. Regional Rivalries:

a. Sunni-Shia Divide: We will explore the historical origins and contemporary implications of the Sunni-Shia divide in the Middle East, including its influence on political alliances, sectarian tensions, and proxy conflicts.

b. Iran-Saudi Arabia Power Struggle: We will examine the power struggle between Iran and Saudi Arabia, discussing their ideological differences, regional ambitions, and the proxy conflicts they are involved in across the Middle East.

c. Other Regional Rivalries: We will also discuss other regional rivalries and conflicts, such as the rivalry between Turkey and Iran, the competition for influence between Qatar and Saudi Arabia, and the ongoing conflicts in Yemen and Syria.

4. Role of External Powers:

a. United States: We will examine the historical and contemporary role of the United States in the Middle East, including its support for authoritarian regimes, interventionist policies, and the impact of U.S. military presence in the region.

b. Russia: We will discuss Russia's reemergence as a major player in the Middle East, its involvement in conflicts such as Syria, and its pursuit of strategic interests in the region.

c. Other External Actors: We will also explore the role of other external powers, including European countries, China, and regional powers such as Turkey and Israel, and their influence on the region's political dynamics.

Conclusion:

The historical and geopolitical factors that have shaped the Middle East have had a profound impact on the region's political landscape. Understanding the complexities of these factors is crucial for comprehending the dynamics of power, conflict, and cooperation in the Middle East. By examining historical legacies, the Arab-Israeli conflict, regional rivalries, and the role of external powers, we gain valuable insights into the complexities of the Middle East's political dynamics and the challenges faced in achieving regional stability and cooperation.

Sunni-Shia Divide and Sectarianism

The Sunni-Shia divide is a significant factor that has shaped the political dynamics of the Middle East for centuries. This section explores the historical roots of the Sunni-Shia divide, its contemporary implications, and the role of sectarianism in the region's conflicts and power struggles.

1. Historical Origins:

a. Early Islamic History: We will provide an overview of the early Islamic period, including the succession dispute after the death of Prophet Muhammad and the emergence of the Sunni and Shia sects.

b. Theological Differences: We will explore the theological and doctrinal differences between Sunni and Shia Islam, such as the question of leadership and the concept of Imamate.

c. Historical Developments: We will examine historical events that deepened the Sunni-Shia divide, including the Battle of Karbala, the Abbasid and Umayyad caliphates, and the Safavid Empire.

2. Contemporary Implications:

a. Demographics and Distribution: We will analyze the distribution of Sunni and Shia populations in the Middle

East, highlighting countries with significant sectarian divides and those with mixed populations.

b. Political Power and Influence: We will discuss the political power dynamics between Sunni-majority and Shia-majority countries, examining the role of sectarian identity in shaping domestic and regional politics.

c. Sectarian Conflicts and Violence: We will explore the sectarian conflicts that have occurred in the region, such as the Iraq War, the Syrian Civil War, and the ongoing tensions in Bahrain and Lebanon, and their implications for regional stability.

3. Sectarianism and Identity Politics:

a. State-Sectarianism Nexus: We will examine how states in the Middle East have instrumentalized sectarianism for political purposes, using it as a tool for maintaining power, suppressing dissent, and mobilizing support.

b. Sectarianism and Identity Formation: We will discuss how sectarian identity intersects with other social, cultural, and political identities in the region, and how it shapes individuals' sense of belonging and political allegiances.

c. Sectarianism and Geopolitical Alliances: We will analyze how sectarianism influences regional alliances and rivalries, such as the Saudi-led Sunni bloc and the Iranianled Shia bloc, and the implications for regional stability and security.

4. Regional Responses and Mitigation Efforts:

a. Interfaith Dialogue and Reconciliation: We will explore efforts at interfaith dialogue and reconciliation, both within and outside the Middle East, aimed at fostering understanding and reducing sectarian tensions.

b. Role of Civil Society: We will discuss the role of civil society organizations, religious leaders, and grassroots movements in promoting dialogue, tolerance, and inclusivity to mitigate sectarianism.

c. Diplomatic and Mediation Efforts: We will examine diplomatic initiatives and mediation efforts by regional and international actors aimed at addressing sectarian conflicts and promoting peaceful coexistence.

Conclusion:

The Sunni-Shia divide and sectarianism have had a profound impact on the Middle East's political dynamics, contributing to conflicts, rivalries, and power struggles in the region. Understanding the historical origins, contemporary implications, and the complex relationship between sectarianism and identity politics is crucial for comprehending the challenges to regional stability and fostering dialogue and reconciliation. Efforts to mitigate sectarian tensions, promote inclusivity, and encourage interfaith dialogue are essential for building a more peaceful and cooperative Middle East.

Arab Spring and Its Aftermath

The Arab Spring was a series of popular uprisings and political protests that swept across the Middle East and North Africa, demanding political reforms, social justice, and greater democratic freedoms. This section examines the causes, dynamics, and consequences of the Arab Spring, including its impact on governance, regional stability, and the rise of non-state actors.

1. Causes and Triggers:

a. Socioeconomic Factors: We will explore the socioeconomic grievances that fueled the Arab Spring, including high unemployment rates, corruption, inequality, and lack of political freedoms.

b. Political Repression and Authoritarian Rule: We will discuss the role of authoritarian regimes and their repressive tactics in triggering popular uprisings, focusing on countries such as Tunisia, Egypt, Libya, Syria, and Yemen.

c. Youth Demographics and Technological Influence: We will analyze the role of youth demographics, the spread of social media, and digital activism in mobilizing and organizing protests during the Arab Spring.

2. Dynamics and Revolutions:

a. Tunisia: We will examine the Tunisian revolution, its origins in the self-immolation of Mohamed Bouazizi, and its successful transition to democracy compared to other countries in the region.

b. Egypt: We will discuss the Egyptian revolution, the role of Tahrir Square as a symbol of protest, and the subsequent political developments, including the rise and fall of the Muslim Brotherhood.

c. Libya, Syria, and Yemen: We will analyze the cases of Libya, Syria, and Yemen, where the initial protests led to protracted conflicts, civil wars, and significant humanitarian crises.

3. Post-Revolutionary Challenges:

a. Political Transitions and Fragile Democracies: We will examine the challenges faced by countries transitioning from authoritarian rule to democracy, including issues of institutional development, constitutional reforms, and power struggles.

b. Rise of Non-State Actors: We will discuss the emergence and role of non-state actors, such as armed militias, extremist groups, and terrorist organizations, and their impact on regional security and stability.

c. Humanitarian and Refugee Crisis: We will explore the humanitarian consequences of the Arab Spring, including the displacement of people, refugee flows, and the strain on neighboring countries and international humanitarian efforts.

4. Regional and Global Implications:

a. Regional Power Shifts: We will analyze the regional power shifts and realignments resulting from the Arab Spring, including the rise of Islamist movements, the rivalry between Saudi Arabia and Iran, and the intervention by external powers.

b. Geopolitical Consequences: We will discuss the geopolitical consequences of the Arab Spring, including the intervention in Libya, the proxy war in Syria, and the impact on regional dynamics, such as the Kurdish question and the Israeli-Palestinian conflict.

c. Lessons Learned: We will reflect on the lessons learned from the Arab Spring, including the challenges of democratization, the importance of inclusive governance, and the need for sustainable economic development.

Conclusion:

The Arab Spring marked a significant turning point in the Middle East's political landscape, with far-reaching consequences that continue to shape the region today. By understanding the causes, dynamics, and aftermath of the Arab Spring, we gain insights into the challenges faced in transitioning to democracy, the rise of non-state actors, and the regional and global implications of these transformative events. The Arab Spring serves as a reminder of the complexities of political change, the need for inclusive governance, and the importance of addressing socioeconomic grievances to achieve long-term stability and prosperity in the Middle East.

Role of Non-State Actors in the Middle East

The Middle East has witnessed the rise and influence of various non-state actors that have significantly shaped the region's political dynamics. This section explores the role of non-state actors, including armed groups, militias, and transnational organizations, and their impact on governance, security, and regional power dynamics.

1. Definition and Types of Non-State Actors:

a. Armed Groups and Militias: We will discuss the emergence and activities of armed groups and militias, both religious and secular, such as Hezbollah, Hamas, the Kurdish groups, and various jihadist organizations.

b. Transnational Organizations: We will explore the role of transnational organizations, such as the Muslim Brotherhood, and their influence across multiple countries in the region.

c. Non-Governmental Organizations (NGOs): We will briefly touch upon the role of non-governmental organizations in the Middle East, focusing on their contributions to social welfare, development, and advocacy.

2. Historical Context and Factors Driving Non-State Actors:

a. Historical Context: We will provide a historical overview of the emergence and evolution of non-state actors in the Middle East, including their origins in anti-colonial struggles, regional conflicts, and power vacuums.

b. Political and Socioeconomic Factors: We will examine the political and socioeconomic factors that have contributed to the rise of non-state actors, including political repression, social inequality, and marginalization.

c. External Support and Proxy Warfare: We will discuss the role of external actors in supporting and exploiting non-state actors as proxies in regional power struggles, such as Iran, Saudi Arabia, and Turkey.

3. Influence on Governance and State Institutions:

a. Governance Challenges: We will explore how non-state actors have challenged the authority and legitimacy of state institutions, often providing alternative governance structures and services in areas under their control.

b. Parallel Systems: We will discuss how non-state actors have established parallel systems of governance, including courts, security forces, and social welfare programs, and the implications for state authority and stability.

c. Delegitimization of State: We will analyze how non-state actors have delegitimized state institutions through propaganda, recruitment, and the provision of social services, eroding state authority and control.

4. Security Dynamics and Regional Power Shifts:

a. Proxy Wars and Regional Conflicts: We will examine the role of non-state actors in proxy wars and regional conflicts, including their influence on the Syrian Civil War, the Yemeni conflict, and the Israeli-Palestinian conflict.

b. Terrorism and Extremism: We will discuss the rise of jihadist groups, their ideology, recruitment strategies, and the security challenges they pose to states in the Middle East and beyond.

c. Impact on Regional Power Dynamics: We will analyze how non-state actors have influenced regional power dynamics, contributing to shifts in alliances, rivalries, and the balance of power between states.

5. Challenges and Responses:

a. Counterterrorism Efforts: We will discuss the counterterrorism strategies employed by states and regional alliances to combat non-state actors, including military operations, intelligence sharing, and counter-radicalization programs.

b. Engagement and Inclusion: We will explore approaches to engaging with non-state actors through dialogue, reconciliation, and political inclusion, highlighting successful cases and their limitations.

c. International Responses: We will examine the role of international actors, such as the United Nations and regional organizations, in addressing the challenges posed by non-state actors and promoting conflict resolution.

Conclusion:

Non-state actors play a significant and complex role in the Middle East, impacting governance, security, and regional power dynamics. Understanding their origins, motivations, and strategies is crucial for comprehending the challenges they pose to state authority, stability, and regional cooperation. Balancing the need to combat extremist groups and maintain security with efforts to address underlying grievances and promote inclusive governance is essential for achieving long-term stability and peace in the Middle East.

Chapter 4: Israeli-Palestinian Conflict
Historical Background and Key Events

The Israeli-Palestinian conflict is a long-standing and complex dispute rooted in competing historical narratives, territorial claims, and national aspirations. This section provides a comprehensive overview of the historical background and key events that have shaped the conflict between Israelis and Palestinians, from the early 20th century to the present day.

1. Early Roots of the Conflict:

a. Ottoman Rule and Zionist Movement: We will explore the rise of the Zionist movement and its goals of establishing a Jewish homeland in Palestine, as well as the impact of Ottoman rule and the Arab response to Zionist settlement.

b. Balfour Declaration and Mandate Period: We will discuss the Balfour Declaration of 1917, which expressed British support for the establishment of a Jewish homeland, and the subsequent British Mandate for Palestine, including its impact on Arab-Jewish relations.

c. Arab Revolts and Palestinian Nationalism: We will examine the Arab revolts against British and Zionist presence in Palestine and the emergence of Palestinian nationalism as a response to Zionist settlement.

2. Partition Plans and the Creation of Israel:

a. United Nations Partition Plan: We will discuss the United Nations' 1947 partition plan, which proposed the division of Palestine into separate Jewish and Arab states, and the subsequent rejection of the plan by Arab countries and Palestinian leadership.

b. 1948 War and Israeli Independence: We will analyze the 1948 Arab-Israeli War, the declaration of the State of Israel, and the displacement of Palestinians, known as the Nakba, which remains a central issue in the conflict.

c. Refugee Issue and Palestinian Identity: We will examine the plight of Palestinian refugees and the development of a distinct Palestinian national identity as a result of the 1948 war and subsequent conflicts.

3. Six-Day War and Occupation:

a. Six-Day War and Occupied Territories: We will discuss the causes and consequences of the 1967 Six-Day War, which resulted in Israeli occupation of the West Bank, Gaza Strip, East Jerusalem, and the Golan Heights.

b. Settlement Expansion and Land Disputes: We will analyze the growth of Israeli settlements in the occupied territories, the legal and political controversies surrounding them, and their impact on the prospects for a two-state solution.

c. Intifadas and Popular Resistance: We will explore the First Intifada (1987-1993) and the Second Intifada (2000-2005), examining the causes, dynamics, and consequences of these popular uprisings against Israeli occupation.

4. Peace Process and Failed Negotiations:

a. Oslo Accords and Peace Process: We will discuss the Oslo Accords of the 1990s, the establishment of the Palestinian Authority, and the subsequent peace negotiations, highlighting the challenges and setbacks faced in achieving a lasting resolution.

b. Camp David Summit and the Second Intifada: We will analyze the Camp David Summit of 2000 and the breakdown of negotiations, leading to the outbreak of the Second Intifada and a period of heightened violence.

c. Failed Peace Initiatives: We will examine other failed peace initiatives, including the Annapolis Conference, the Road Map for Peace, and the efforts of the Quartet (United States, European Union, United Nations, and Russia) to mediate the conflict.

5. Recent Developments and Current Status:

a. Gaza Disengagement and Hamas Rule: We will discuss the 2005 Israeli disengagement from the Gaza Strip, the subsequent rise of Hamas, and the challenges posed by the division of governance between Hamas in Gaza and the Palestinian Authority in the West Bank.

b. Settlement Expansion and Annexation Plans: We will analyze recent Israeli policies regarding settlement expansion, the proposed annexation of parts of the West Bank, and their implications for the viability of a two-state solution.

c. International Efforts and Regional Dynamics: We will examine international initiatives and regional dynamics, including the role of Arab states, in seeking to revive the peace process and address the core issues of the conflict.

Conclusion:

The historical background and key events of the Israeli-Palestinian conflict provide a crucial foundation for understanding the complexities and challenges of achieving a just and lasting resolution. Recognizing the narratives, grievances, and aspirations of both Israelis and Palestinians is essential for fostering dialogue, reconciliation, and a pathway towards peace and coexistence.

Territorial Disputes and Settlements

Territorial disputes and the issue of settlements are among the most contentious and complex aspects of the Israeli-Palestinian conflict. This section delves into the history, dynamics, and implications of territorial disputes, including the establishment and expansion of Israeli settlements in the occupied territories.

1. Historical Context of Territorial Disputes:

a. Pre-1948 Borders and Partition Plans: We will examine the pre-1948 borders of Palestine and the various partition plans proposed before the establishment of the State of Israel, including the 1947 United Nations Partition Plan.

b. Armistice Lines and Occupied Territories: We will discuss the armistice lines drawn after the 1948 Arab-Israeli War, which led to the occupation of the West Bank, Gaza Strip, and East Jerusalem by Jordan and Egypt, and their subsequent capture by Israel in the 1967 Six-Day War.

c. Status of Jerusalem: We will analyze the historical and religious significance of Jerusalem, the competing claims of Israelis and Palestinians, and the international community's stance on the city's status.

2. Israeli Settlement Policies:

a. Settlement Expansion and Israeli Perspectives: We will explore the motivations and perspectives behind Israeli settlement policies, including the ideological, security, and demographic factors that drive the establishment and growth of settlements.

b. Settlement Construction Process: We will discuss the process of settlement construction, including the role of Israeli government agencies, settlement organizations, and the legal framework that facilitates the expansion of settlements.

c. Settlement Outposts and Unauthorized Construction: We will examine the issue of settlement outposts, which are often established without official approval, and their impact on the territorial contiguity of a future Palestinian state.

3. International Law and Settlements:

a. Legal Perspectives on Settlements: We will analyze the international legal framework, including United Nations resolutions, the Fourth Geneva Convention, and the International Court of Justice's advisory opinion on settlements, to assess the legality of Israeli settlements.

b. International Condemnation and Diplomatic Responses: We will discuss the international community's condemnation of Israeli settlements, the positions of various countries and regional organizations, and the diplomatic efforts to halt settlement expansion.

c. Economic and Humanitarian Impact on Palestinians: We will examine the economic and humanitarian consequences of settlements on the daily lives of Palestinians, including restrictions on movement, access to natural resources, and land confiscation.

4. Challenges to the Two-State Solution:

a. Implications for a Two-State Solution: We will analyze the impact of settlement expansion on the feasibility of a two-state solution, including its effect on the contiguity of Palestinian territories and the viability of East Jerusalem as the future capital of a Palestinian state.

b. Israeli-Palestinian Negotiations and Settlements: We will examine how settlements have been a major obstacle in Israeli-Palestinian negotiations, often leading to deadlock and frustration.

c. Alternatives and Controversial Proposals: We will explore alternative proposals, such as land swaps or the annexation of settlements, and the controversies surrounding these ideas.

5. Regional and International Efforts to Address Settlements:

a. Role of the United States: We will analyze the role of the United States in addressing settlements, including its policy shifts over the years and the impact of its positions on the peace process.

b. International Initiatives and Boycott Movements: We will discuss international initiatives, such as the Boycott, Divestment, and Sanctions (BDS) movement, aimed at pressuring Israel to halt settlement construction and the controversies surrounding these efforts.

c. Peace Process and Settlements: We will examine how settlements have been a central issue in Israeli-Palestinian peace negotiations and the challenges faced in reaching a comprehensive agreement that addresses territorial disputes.

Conclusion:

Territorial disputes and settlements are deeply intertwined with the Israeli-Palestinian conflict, shaping the landscape of the occupied territories and posing significant challenges to the prospects of a peaceful resolution. Addressing the complexities of territorial issues and settlement expansion requires political will, dialogue, and a commitment to finding a mutually acceptable solution that respects the rights and aspirations of both Israelis and Palestinians.

Peace Process and Two-State Solution

The pursuit of a two-state solution has been a central goal of the Israeli-Palestinian peace process. This section explores the historical context, challenges, and prospects of achieving a negotiated settlement that leads to the establishment of an independent Palestinian state alongside Israel.

1. Historical Context of the Peace Process:

a. Oslo Accords and the Peace Process Beginnings: We will discuss the significance of the Oslo Accords, signed in 1993, as a pivotal moment in Israeli-Palestinian negotiations and the establishment of a framework for the peace process.

b. Previous Negotiations and Peace Initiatives: We will examine previous attempts at peace negotiations, such as the Camp David Summit in 2000 and the Annapolis Conference in 2007, and analyze their impact on the peace process.

c. Key Milestones and Agreements: We will highlight important agreements and initiatives, including the Road Map for Peace, the Arab Peace Initiative, and the efforts of the Quartet, comprising the United States, the United Nations, the European Union, and Russia.

2. Core Issues in the Peace Process:

a. Borders and Territorial Arrangements: We will delve into the challenges surrounding border delineation, including the status of Jerusalem, the division of land, and the issue of Israeli settlements.

b. Security and Defense Arrangements: We will examine the complex task of addressing security concerns for both Israelis and Palestinians, including demilitarization, border control, and counterterrorism cooperation.

c. Refugees and the Right of Return: We will discuss the issue of Palestinian refugees and their right of return, exploring the historical context, different perspectives, and potential solutions.

d. Water and Natural Resources: We will analyze the complexities of water allocation and management, as well as the potential for cooperation and joint management of shared resources.

3. Challenges and Obstacles in the Peace Process:

a. Trust-Building and Confidence-Building Measures: We will explore the importance of trust-building and confidence-building measures in fostering an environment conducive to negotiations and long-term peace.

b. Political Divisions and Intra-Palestinian Dynamics: We will examine the impact of internal divisions among

Palestinian factions, such as Fatah and Hamas, on the peace process and the quest for Palestinian unity.

c. Israeli Domestic Politics and Settlements: We will discuss how domestic political considerations in Israel, including the influence of settlement proponents, can pose challenges to the advancement of the peace process.

d. Regional Dynamics and External Actors: We will analyze the role of regional dynamics and external actors, including neighboring Arab states and international powers, in shaping the peace process and their potential influence on its outcomes.

4. International Diplomatic Efforts and Mediation:

a. Role of the United States: We will assess the historical role of the United States as a mediator in the peace process, examining different approaches and the impact of shifting administrations.

b. Involvement of International Organizations: We will explore the contributions of international organizations, such as the United Nations and the European Union, in supporting the peace process and facilitating negotiations.

c. Track II Diplomacy and Civil Society Initiatives: We will discuss the importance of Track II diplomacy and civil society initiatives in promoting dialogue, fostering mutual understanding, and bridging gaps between Israelis and Palestinians.

5. Prospects for the Two-State Solution:

a. Emerging Alternatives and One-State Scenarios: We will examine emerging alternatives to the two-state solution, including proposals for a confederation or a binational state, and analyze their feasibility and implications.

b. Public Opinion and Popular Support: We will assess the public opinion dynamics among Israelis and Palestinians regarding the two-state solution and the challenges of garnering widespread support.

c. Lessons from Successful Peace Processes: We will draw lessons from successful peace processes in other regions, such as Northern Ireland and South Africa, and explore how these experiences can inform the Israeli-Palestinian context.

Conclusion:

Achieving a two-state solution to the Israeli-Palestinian conflict remains a complex and challenging endeavor. It requires a sustained commitment to dialogue, compromise, and addressing the core issues at the heart of the conflict. While obstacles persist, the pursuit of peace, justice, and security for both Israelis and Palestinians is essential for a peaceful and sustainable future in the region.

International Perspectives and Mediation Efforts

The Israeli-Palestinian conflict has garnered significant attention and involvement from the international community. This section explores the diverse perspectives of key international actors and their efforts in mediating the conflict, as well as the challenges and opportunities they face.

1. United Nations and the Israeli-Palestinian Conflict:

a. Historical Background and Resolutions: We will provide an overview of the United Nations' involvement in the Israeli-Palestinian conflict, including key resolutions and initiatives aimed at promoting peace, addressing humanitarian concerns, and upholding international law.

b. Role of UN Agencies and Special Envoys: We will examine the contributions of UN agencies, such as UNRWA, in providing assistance to Palestinian refugees, as well as the role of special envoys and mediators appointed by the United Nations.

c. Security Council and General Assembly Dynamics: We will analyze the dynamics within the UN Security Council and General Assembly concerning the Israeli-Palestinian conflict, including debates, voting patterns, and the impact of veto powers.

2. United States and Its Mediation Role:

a. Historical Role and Policy Shifts: We will explore the historical role of the United States as a key mediator in the Israeli-Palestinian conflict, examining different approaches and policy shifts over time.

b. Camp David Accords and Subsequent Efforts: We will discuss the significance of the Camp David Accords in 1978 and subsequent US-led efforts, such as the Oslo Accords and the Annapolis Conference, in advancing the peace process.

c. Evolving US-Israel Relationship: We will analyze the evolving relationship between the United States and Israel, considering its influence on US mediation efforts and the perceptions of impartiality.

3. European Union and Its Mediation Initiatives:

a. EU Policy Positions and Declarations: We will examine the European Union's policy positions on the Israeli-Palestinian conflict, including its support for a two-state solution, human rights, and adherence to international law.

b. Economic and Political Engagement: We will discuss the EU's economic and political engagement with both Israelis and Palestinians, exploring initiatives aimed at promoting dialogue, reconciliation, and state-building efforts.

c. Quartet and Multilateral Diplomacy: We will analyze the role of the EU as part of the Quartet, comprising the United States, the United Nations, and Russia, in facilitating multilateral diplomacy and advancing the peace process.

4. Arab League and Regional Mediation Efforts:

a. Arab Peace Initiative: We will discuss the Arab Peace Initiative, launched in 2002, which offers a comprehensive peace plan in exchange for Israel's withdrawal from the occupied territories and the establishment of a Palestinian state.

b. Jordan and Egypt as Mediators: We will examine the mediation roles of Jordan and Egypt, two key Arab states with peace treaties with Israel, and their efforts in facilitating dialogue and negotiations.

c. Gulf Cooperation Council (GCC) Engagement: We will explore the growing engagement of Gulf states, such as Saudi Arabia and the United Arab Emirates, in regional diplomacy and their potential influence on the Israeli-Palestinian conflict.

5. Other International Actors and Initiatives:

a. Russia's Mediation Efforts: We will assess Russia's involvement in mediating the Israeli-Palestinian conflict, including its role in hosting summits and promoting dialogue between the parties.

b. Non-Governmental Organizations (NGOs) and Civil Society: We will discuss the contributions of NGOs and civil society organizations in promoting peace, dialogue, and grassroots initiatives, highlighting examples of successful mediation efforts.

c. International Peacebuilding and Conflict Resolution Mechanisms: We will examine the role of international peacebuilding and conflict resolution mechanisms, such as the International Criminal Court (ICC) and various international tribunals, in addressing accountability and promoting reconciliation.

Conclusion:

International perspectives and mediation efforts play a crucial role in advancing the Israeli-Palestinian peace process. The involvement of key international actors, including the United Nations, the United States, the European Union, and regional players, offers both challenges and opportunities for finding a just and lasting resolution to the conflict. The commitment of the international community to support dialogue, foster understanding, and address the core issues will be instrumental in achieving a peaceful and sustainable solution.

Chapter 5: Regional Rivalries in the Middle East
Iran-Saudi Arabia Power Struggle

The Middle East has long been characterized by regional rivalries that shape its political dynamics. One of the most prominent and consequential rivalries in the region is between Iran and Saudi Arabia. This section delves into the complexities of the Iran-Saudi Arabia power struggle, exploring its historical context, ideological dimensions, geopolitical implications, and impact on regional stability.

1. Historical Context:

a. Origins of the Rivalry: We will provide a historical overview of the factors that have contributed to the Iran-Saudi Arabia power struggle, including religious, political, and ideological differences.

b. Iran's Islamic Revolution: We will examine the 1979 Islamic Revolution in Iran and its impact on the dynamics of the power struggle, including the emergence of Iran as a revolutionary Islamist state challenging the traditional Saudi-led order.

c. Sectarian Dimensions: We will explore how the Sunni-Shia divide has played a role in exacerbating tensions between Iran and Saudi Arabia, highlighting incidents and conflicts that have fueled sectarian animosities.

2. Ideological and Geopolitical Dimensions:

a. Shia Crescent and Sunni Counterbalance: We will discuss the concept of the "Shia Crescent" and its implications for Saudi Arabia's regional standing, as well as the efforts by Saudi Arabia and its allies to counterbalance Iran's influence.

b. Proxy Conflicts and Support for Non-State Actors: We will analyze the role of proxy conflicts in the power struggle, examining instances where Iran and Saudi Arabia have supported non-state actors in conflicts across the region, such as in Yemen, Iraq, Syria, and Lebanon.

c. Geopolitical Competition: We will explore the geopolitical competition between Iran and Saudi Arabia for regional influence, including their involvement in regional organizations, alliances, and attempts to establish spheres of influence.

3. Regional Impact:

a. Yemen Crisis: We will delve into the Yemeni Civil War and its significance as a major theater of the Iran-Saudi Arabia power struggle, examining the motivations, interests, and interventions of both sides in the conflict.

b. Sectarianism and Destabilization: We will analyze how the Iran-Saudi Arabia power struggle has fueled sectarian tensions and contributed to the destabilization of countries in the region, exacerbating conflicts and hindering stability.

c. Gulf Cooperation Council (GCC) Dynamics: We will discuss the impact of the Iran-Saudi Arabia power struggle on the Gulf Cooperation Council (GCC), a regional organization comprising Arab Gulf states, and the efforts to maintain unity and coherence in the face of diverging interests.

4. International Dimensions:

a. United States and Western Powers: We will examine the role of the United States and Western powers in navigating the Iran-Saudi Arabia power struggle, including their alliances, security commitments, and attempts to mitigate tensions.

b. Russia and China: We will assess the involvement of Russia and China in the power struggle, exploring their geopolitical interests, economic engagements, and attempts to leverage the rivalry for their own benefit.

c. International Mediation and De-escalation Efforts: We will discuss international mediation and de-escalation efforts aimed at reducing tensions between Iran and Saudi Arabia, including diplomatic initiatives and Track II dialogues.

Conclusion:

The Iran-Saudi Arabia power struggle represents a significant regional rivalry in the Middle East with far-reaching implications. Understanding the historical context, ideological dimensions, and geopolitical dynamics of this rivalry is crucial for comprehending the regional landscape and working towards sustainable peace and stability. Efforts to de-escalate tensions and find common ground between Iran and Saudi Arabia, as well as regional and international actors, are essential for fostering a more cooperative and secure Middle East.

Proxy Conflicts and Sectarian Tensions

Proxy conflicts and sectarian tensions have played a significant role in shaping the regional rivalries in the Middle East. This section explores the dynamics of proxy conflicts and their connection to sectarian tensions, highlighting their impact on the stability and security of the region.

1. Historical Context:

a. Cold War Influence: We will examine how the Cold War rivalry between the United States and the Soviet Union contributed to the emergence of proxy conflicts in the Middle East, including their support for different factions and ideologies.

b. Sectarianism and Regional Dynamics: We will explore the historical roots of sectarian tensions in the region, tracing the influence of religious, political, and social factors on the development of sectarian identities and rivalries.

c. Iran-Iraq War: We will analyze the Iran-Iraq War (1980-1988) as a pivotal moment in proxy conflicts and sectarian tensions, examining how regional and international actors were involved and how sectarian dynamics influenced the conflict.

2. Proxy Conflicts:

a. Yemen: We will delve into the Yemeni Civil War, which has become a proxy battleground between regional powers, particularly Saudi Arabia and Iran, analyzing the motivations, interests, and support provided to the different factions involved.

b. Syria: We will discuss the Syrian Civil War and the complex web of proxy conflicts, involving various regional and international actors, and how sectarian dimensions have fueled the intensity and longevity of the conflict.

c. Iraq: We will examine the post-2003 Iraq War and the subsequent insurgency, focusing on the proxy conflicts and sectarian tensions that emerged as different factions vied for power and influence.

3. Sectarian Tensions:

a. Sunni-Shia Divide: We will analyze the historical and ideological factors underlying the Sunni-Shia divide, exploring how this sectarian tension has been exploited by regional actors to advance their geopolitical agendas.

b. Sectarianism in Bahrain: We will discuss the sectarian tensions in Bahrain, highlighting the marginalized Shia population and the protests that erupted during the Arab Spring, as well as the involvement of external actors in the country's internal dynamics.

c. Sectarianism in Lebanon: We will examine the sectarian dynamics in Lebanon, focusing on the role of Hezbollah, a Shia political and military organization, and its relationship with other sectarian groups, as well as external influences.

4. Impact and Consequences:

a. Humanitarian Crisis: We will address the humanitarian consequences of proxy conflicts and sectarian tensions, discussing the displacement of populations, the destruction of infrastructure, and the challenges in providing aid and assistance to affected areas.

b. Regional Stability: We will analyze the impact of proxy conflicts and sectarian tensions on regional stability, including the spillover effects, the exacerbation of existing conflicts, and the potential for further escalation.

c. Counterterrorism Efforts: We will discuss how proxy conflicts and sectarian tensions have influenced counterterrorism efforts in the region, examining the complex dynamics between terrorist organizations, state actors, and regional rivalries.

Conclusion:

Proxy conflicts and sectarian tensions have become entrenched features of the regional rivalries in the Middle East. Understanding the historical context, geopolitical interests, and sectarian dynamics is crucial for comprehending the complexities of these conflicts and their impact on the stability and security of the region. Efforts to address the root causes of sectarian tensions, promote dialogue, and find political solutions are essential for reducing the influence of proxy conflicts and fostering a more peaceful and inclusive Middle East.

Role of External Powers in Regional Dynamics

The Middle East has long been a theater for the involvement of external powers, whose interests and interventions have shaped the regional dynamics and rivalries. This section examines the role of external powers in the Middle East, exploring their motivations, strategies, and impact on the stability and security of the region.

1. Historical Context:

a. Colonial Legacies: We will discuss the historical legacies of colonialism in the Middle East and how they have influenced the involvement of external powers in the region, including the division of territories, the establishment of client states, and the exploitation of resources.

b. Cold War Influence: We will analyze the Cold War era and its impact on the Middle East, examining how the United States and the Soviet Union competed for influence, supported regional allies, and fueled rivalries through military aid and interventions.

2. Major External Powers:

a. United States: We will examine the role of the United States as a major external power in the Middle East, discussing its strategic interests, military presence, and alliances with regional actors. We will also explore the evolving dynamics of U.S. policy towards the region, including the impact of the war on terror and recent shifts in geopolitical priorities.

b. Russia: We will discuss Russia's resurgence as an influential player in the Middle East, analyzing its military interventions, alliances, and economic engagements with regional actors. We will also explore Russia's motivations and objectives in the region, including its pursuit of energy resources, geopolitical influence, and countering Western dominance.

c. China: We will assess China's growing presence and interests in the Middle East, examining its economic investments, energy partnerships, and Belt and Road Initiative. We will discuss China's approach to regional dynamics, its relationships with key players, and its efforts to expand its influence in the region.

3. Strategies and Motivations:

a. Geopolitical Interests: We will analyze the geopolitical interests of external powers in the Middle East, including access to resources, control over strategic locations, and countering the influence of rival powers.

b. Security Concerns: We will discuss the security considerations that drive external powers' involvement in the region, such as the fight against terrorism, the proliferation of weapons of mass destruction, and the protection of their national interests.

c. Economic and Energy Factors: We will examine the economic and energy factors that shape the involvement of external powers in the Middle East, including access to oil and gas resources, trade relations, and investment opportunities.

4. Impact on Regional Dynamics:

a. Proxy Conflicts and Regional Rivalries: We will analyze how the involvement of external powers in regional conflicts and rivalries has fueled instability, exacerbated sectarian tensions, and prolonged conflicts, examining specific examples such as Syria, Yemen, and Iraq.

b. Balancing Acts: We will discuss the efforts of regional actors to balance the influence of external powers, including strategic alliances, diplomatic engagements, and diversification of partnerships.

c. Implications for Regional Security: We will examine the implications of the role of external powers on regional security, including the potential for further destabilization, arms race dynamics, and the challenges of achieving sustainable peace and stability.

Conclusion:

The involvement of external powers in the Middle East has had a profound impact on the regional dynamics and rivalries. Understanding their motivations, strategies, and interests is crucial for comprehending the complexities of the regional landscape and working towards a more stable and secure Middle East. Efforts to promote dialogue, cooperation, and inclusive regional frameworks are essential for managing the influence of external powers and fostering a sustainable and peaceful future for the region.

Impact of Regional Rivalries on Stability and Security

The Middle East has been characterized by a complex web of regional rivalries, with competing powers vying for influence, resources, and dominance. This section delves into the impact of these rivalries on the stability and security of the region, examining their causes, manifestations, and consequences.

1. Causes and Dynamics of Regional Rivalries:

a. Historical Context: We will provide a historical overview of the roots of regional rivalries in the Middle East, including territorial disputes, ideological differences, and power struggles among key actors.

b. Geopolitical Interests: We will analyze the geopolitical interests of regional powers and how they contribute to the emergence and perpetuation of rivalries, focusing on issues such as access to resources, control of strategic locations, and pursuit of regional hegemony.

c. Sectarian and Ethno-Religious Divisions: We will explore how sectarian and ethno-religious divisions, particularly the Sunni-Shia divide, contribute to regional rivalries, examining how these divisions are exploited by competing powers to advance their interests and influence.

2. Manifestations of Regional Rivalries:

a. Proxy Conflicts: We will examine how regional rivalries manifest in the form of proxy conflicts, where competing powers support and arm different factions within a country to further their own interests. Case studies such as the conflicts in Syria, Yemen, and Libya will be analyzed.

b. Sectarian Tensions: We will discuss how regional rivalries exacerbate sectarian tensions, fueling sectarian conflicts and deepening divisions within societies. Examples such as the Sunni-Shia rivalry and its impact on Iraq and Lebanon will be explored.

c. Economic Competition: We will analyze how economic competition between regional powers contributes to rivalries, focusing on sectors such as oil and gas, trade, and investment. We will discuss how economic rivalries impact regional stability and development.

3. Consequences for Stability and Security:

a. Humanitarian Crisis: We will examine the humanitarian consequences of regional rivalries, including the displacement of populations, the destruction of infrastructure, and the worsening of living conditions for affected communities.

b. Regional Fragmentation: We will discuss how regional rivalries contribute to the fragmentation of the Middle East, with competing powers seeking to establish spheres of influence and support their preferred factions, resulting in divided loyalties and fractured political landscapes.

    c. Arms Proliferation: We will analyze how regional rivalries contribute to the proliferation of arms and weapons in the region, fueling conflicts and increasing the risk of escalation and instability.

    d. Impediment to Conflict Resolution: We will explore how regional rivalries hinder efforts to achieve peaceful resolutions to conflicts, as competing powers often prioritize their own interests over the broader goal of stability and peace.

    4. International Efforts and Mediation:

    a. International Diplomatic Initiatives: We will discuss the role of international actors and organizations in mediating regional rivalries and promoting dialogue, examining the effectiveness and challenges of such initiatives.

    b. Impact of External Powers: We will analyze how the involvement of external powers in the region, such as the United States, Russia, and China, affects regional rivalries and the prospects for stability and security.

    c. Role of Regional Organizations: We will examine the role of regional organizations, such as the Arab League and the Gulf Cooperation Council, in mitigating regional rivalries and fostering cooperation among member states.

Conclusion:

The regional rivalries in the Middle East have far-reaching implications for stability and security. The complex interplay of geopolitical interests, sectarian tensions, and economic competition fuels conflicts, exacerbates divisions, and hampers efforts towards peace and development. Resolving regional rivalries requires a comprehensive approach that addresses the root causes, engages all relevant stakeholders, and promotes inclusive dialogue and cooperation. International and regional actors must work together to de-escalate tensions, facilitate conflict resolution, and foster a more stable and secure Middle East.

Chapter 6: Oil Politics and Resource Curse

Importance of Oil in Middle Eastern Politics

The Middle East is widely recognized as a region of strategic importance due to its abundant oil reserves. This section explores the significance of oil in shaping the politics of the Middle East, examining how it influences domestic and international dynamics, economic development, and power relations.

1. Historical Context:

a. Discovery of Oil: We will provide a historical overview of the discovery of oil in the Middle East and its impact on the region's political landscape. This includes key events, such as the establishment of national oil companies and the rise of oil-dependent economies.

b. Geopolitical Significance: We will discuss the geopolitical significance of Middle Eastern oil, including its role in shaping international relations, regional conflicts, and the interests of external powers.

2. Economic Dimensions:

a. Oil Production and Revenue: We will analyze the economic importance of oil production in the Middle East, exploring the scale of production, revenue generation, and its contribution to national budgets.

b. Economic Dependency: We will discuss the challenges associated with oil dependency, including the vulnerability of economies to fluctuations in oil prices, limited diversification, and the impact on employment, income distribution, and social welfare.

c. Rentier States: We will examine the concept of rentier states and how oil wealth shapes the social and political dynamics within these countries, including the relationship between the state and its citizens.

3. Political Power and Governance:

a. Petrostates and Authoritarianism: We will explore the linkages between oil wealth and authoritarian governance in the Middle East, discussing how resource revenues can be used to consolidate political power and suppress dissent.

b. Rent-Seeking and Corruption: We will analyze the phenomenon of rent-seeking and corruption in oil-rich countries, examining how the abundance of natural resources can undermine governance, transparency, and accountability.

c. Resource Nationalism: We will discuss the role of resource nationalism in Middle Eastern politics, examining how states assert control over their oil resources, negotiate contracts with international oil companies, and shape the terms of engagement with the global energy market.

4. Geopolitics and International Relations:

a. OPEC and Oil Diplomacy: We will explore the role of the Organization of the Petroleum Exporting Countries (OPEC) in Middle Eastern oil politics, discussing how the organization influences global oil prices, coordinates production levels, and acts as a platform for diplomatic negotiations among member states.

b. Energy Security and Geopolitical Competition: We will analyze the geopolitical implications of Middle Eastern oil for energy security, focusing on the interests and rivalries of major powers in the region, including the United States, Russia, China, and European countries.

c. Oil and Conflict: We will examine the relationship between oil and conflict in the Middle East, discussing how control over oil resources can be a driving factor in regional conflicts, as well as the challenges of resource management in conflict-affected areas.

5. Environmental and Sustainable Development Challenges:

a. Environmental Impact: We will discuss the environmental consequences of oil extraction and production in the Middle East, including pollution, greenhouse gas emissions, and the challenges of transitioning to cleaner energy sources.

b. Diversification and Sustainable Development: We will explore the imperative for oil-dependent economies to diversify their economies and promote sustainable development, discussing efforts to develop non-oil sectors, foster innovation, and enhance human capital.

c. The Transition to Renewable Energy: We will examine the opportunities and challenges of transitioning from oil to renewable energy sources in the Middle East, including the potential for regional cooperation, investment in renewable infrastructure, and the role of technology and innovation.

Conclusion:

Oil plays a central role in shaping the politics, economy, and international relations of the Middle East. While it has brought wealth and power to some countries, it has also presented challenges such as economic dependency, corruption, and environmental degradation. The region's future hinges on its ability to manage its oil resources sustainably, diversify its economies, and adapt to a changing global energy landscape.

Resource Curse Phenomenon and Economic Challenges

The resource curse, also known as the paradox of plenty, refers to the phenomenon where countries rich in natural resources, such as oil, minerals, or gas, experience economic challenges and underdevelopment instead of reaping the benefits of their resource wealth. This section explores the resource curse in the context of the Middle East, focusing on the economic challenges associated with oil politics and the potential solutions to overcome them.

1. Understanding the Resource Curse:

a. Definition and Characteristics: We will define the resource curse and discuss its key characteristics, including the negative impact on economic growth, governance, social development, and the environment.

b. Historical Examples: We will provide historical examples of resource curse phenomena in the Middle East, examining cases where countries have struggled to translate their resource wealth into sustainable economic development.

2. Economic Challenges of the Resource Curse:

a. Dutch Disease: We will explain the concept of the Dutch Disease, discussing how the overreliance on oil exports can lead to a decline in other sectors of the economy, such as manufacturing and agriculture.

b. Volatility and Uncertainty: We will explore the economic challenges posed by the volatility of oil prices and the uncertainty surrounding future oil reserves, including the impact on fiscal planning, investment decisions, and economic stability.

c. Rentier Economy: We will analyze the characteristics of a rentier economy, where the state derives a significant portion of its revenue from rent, such as oil rents, and the challenges associated with this economic model.

3. Governance and Institutional Challenges:

a. Rent-Seeking and Corruption: We will discuss how resource wealth can incentivize rent-seeking behavior and foster corruption, undermining governance, accountability, and public trust.

b. Weak Institutions: We will examine the impact of the resource curse on institutions and governance structures, discussing how the concentration of power and wealth can hinder the development of robust institutions, the rule of law, and effective public service delivery.

c. Lack of Economic Diversification: We will explore the challenge of economic diversification in resource-rich countries, discussing the barriers and risks associated with transitioning to non-resource sectors, such as manufacturing, services, or innovation-based industries.

4. Managing Resource Wealth:

a. Fiscal Policy and Stabilization Funds: We will analyze the role of fiscal policies, including the establishment of stabilization funds, in managing resource revenues, mitigating the impact of oil price volatility, and investing in sustainable development.

b. Sovereign Wealth Funds: We will discuss the importance of sovereign wealth funds as vehicles for long-term investment, economic diversification, and intergenerational equity, examining successful examples from the Middle East.

c. Transparency and Accountability: We will explore the significance of transparency and accountability measures in resource-rich countries, such as the publication of oil contracts, revenue transparency initiatives, and the role of civil society and media in monitoring resource governance.

5. Strategies for Economic Transformation:

a. Economic Diversification: We will discuss the imperative of economic diversification as a strategy to overcome the resource curse, exploring successful diversification models from other regions and potential sectors for diversification in the Middle East.

b. Human Capital Development: We will examine the importance of investing in human capital, education, and skills development to foster innovation, entrepreneurship, and a knowledge-based economy.

c. Sustainable Development Goals: We will discuss how aligning resource-rich economies with the United Nations Sustainable Development Goals (SDGs) can provide a framework for inclusive and sustainable development, including poverty alleviation, environmental sustainability, and social progress.

Conclusion:

The resource curse poses significant economic challenges for resource-rich countries in the Middle East. However, by implementing effective governance mechanisms, pursuing economic diversification, and investing in human capital, it is possible to mitigate the negative impacts of the resource curse and achieve sustainable economic development. The successful management of oil politics and the avoidance of the resource curse can lead to a more prosperous and resilient future for the Middle East.

Diversification and Sustainable Development

Diversification and sustainable development are key strategies for resource-rich countries in the Middle East to overcome the challenges posed by the resource curse and achieve long-term economic stability. This section explores the importance of diversification, the potential sectors for diversification, and the integration of sustainable development principles into the economic fabric of oil-rich nations.

1. Understanding Diversification:

a. Definition and Rationale: We will define economic diversification and explain why it is crucial for resource-rich countries, particularly in the Middle East, to reduce their dependence on oil revenues and develop robust and diverse economies.

b. Benefits of Diversification: We will discuss the potential benefits of economic diversification, including reduced vulnerability to oil price volatility, increased employment opportunities, enhanced productivity, and the promotion of innovation and entrepreneurship.

2. Sectors for Diversification:

a. Manufacturing and Industrialization: We will explore the potential of manufacturing and industrial sectors as avenues for economic diversification, discussing the necessary infrastructure, policies, and investments to foster their growth.

b. Services and Tourism: We will examine the role of services, including financial services, information technology, and tourism, in diversifying the economies of resource-rich countries, highlighting successful examples from the region.

c. Innovation and Knowledge-Based Industries: We will discuss the significance of fostering innovation, research and development, and knowledge-based industries as drivers of economic diversification and sustainable development.

3. Overcoming Challenges:

a. Institutional and Policy Reforms: We will analyze the institutional and policy reforms required to facilitate economic diversification, including the simplification of regulatory frameworks, improvements in business environments, and the promotion of entrepreneurship and private sector development.

b. Infrastructure Development: We will explore the importance of infrastructure development, such as transportation, telecommunications, and energy, in supporting economic diversification and attracting investments in non-resource sectors.

c. Human Capital Development: We will discuss the critical role of human capital development, education, and skills training in building a diversified and knowledge-based economy, focusing on the need to nurture talent and foster a culture of innovation.

4. Integrating Sustainable Development:

a. Environmental Considerations: We will examine the importance of integrating environmental sustainability into the diversification process, discussing strategies for reducing carbon emissions, promoting renewable energy sources, and adopting green technologies.

b. Social Inclusion: We will explore the significance of social inclusion in the diversification agenda, addressing issues of income inequality, gender equality, and the inclusion of marginalized communities in the economic development process.

c. Governance and Transparency: We will discuss the role of good governance, transparency, and accountability in promoting sustainable development, including the management of natural resources, public finances, and the equitable distribution of benefits.

5. International Cooperation and Partnerships:

a. Foreign Direct Investment: We will examine the role of foreign direct investment (FDI) in supporting economic diversification, including the attraction of foreign capital, technology transfer, and the creation of strategic partnerships with international companies.

b. Regional Integration: We will discuss the potential benefits of regional integration, such as trade agreements and economic alliances, in promoting economic diversification, enhancing market access, and fostering cooperation among resource-rich countries.

c. Sustainable Development Goals (SDGs): We will explore how aligning diversification efforts with the United Nations Sustainable Development Goals can provide a framework for inclusive and sustainable development, including poverty reduction, education, health, and environmental sustainability.

Conclusion:

Diversification and sustainable development are essential strategies for resource-rich countries in the Middle East to overcome the challenges of the resource curse and achieve long-term economic stability. By diversifying their economies, investing in key sectors, integrating sustainable development principles, and fostering international cooperation, these countries can build resilient and prosperous economies that are less vulnerable to oil price fluctuations and contribute to the well-being of their societies.

Implications of Changing Energy Landscape

The global energy landscape is undergoing significant transformations, with shifts in energy sources, technology advancements, and increasing concerns about climate change. This section explores the implications of these changes for oil-rich countries in the Middle East, focusing on the challenges and opportunities they face in adapting to a rapidly evolving energy environment.

1. The Transition to Renewable Energy:

a. Growing Demand for Renewable Energy: We will discuss the increasing global demand for renewable energy sources, driven by environmental concerns, energy security, and technological advancements. This shift poses challenges for oil-rich countries heavily reliant on fossil fuel exports.

b. Impact on Oil Demand: We will examine the potential implications of the growing adoption of renewable energy on oil demand, including the projected decrease in demand for fossil fuels and the potential impact on oil prices and revenues.

c. Economic Diversification: We will explore how the transition to renewable energy presents opportunities for oil-rich countries to diversify their economies by investing in renewable energy technologies, manufacturing, and related industries.

2. Technological Advancements and Energy Efficiency:

a. Advancements in Energy Efficiency: We will discuss the importance of energy efficiency measures in reducing energy consumption and mitigating the environmental impact of energy production and consumption. We will explore the potential for technology advancements to improve energy efficiency in various sectors, including transportation, buildings, and industry.

b. Innovation and Research: We will highlight the role of innovation, research and development, and technology transfer in driving energy efficiency improvements, and the potential for oil-rich countries to invest in these areas to enhance their competitiveness in the evolving energy landscape.

3. Environmental and Climate Considerations:

a. Climate Change and Emission Reduction Goals: We will examine the increasing global focus on mitigating climate change and reducing greenhouse gas emissions. We will discuss the implications for oil-rich countries, including the need to address their carbon footprint and transition towards low-carbon energy systems.

b. Carbon Pricing and Environmental Regulations: We will explore the potential impact of carbon pricing mechanisms and environmental regulations on the oil industry, including the costs and challenges associated with compliance and the opportunities for developing carbon capture and storage technologies.

c. Renewable Energy Integration: We will discuss the challenges and opportunities of integrating renewable energy sources into existing energy infrastructure, including grid modernization, energy storage solutions, and the development of smart grids.

4. Geopolitical Shifts and Energy Security:

a. Geopolitical Implications: We will examine the geopolitical implications of the changing energy landscape, including shifts in global energy power dynamics, the potential for energy market disruptions, and the changing roles of oil-rich countries in global energy governance.

b. Energy Security Strategies: We will explore the strategies that oil-rich countries can adopt to enhance their energy security in a changing energy landscape, including diversifying their energy sources, investing in renewable energy technologies, and developing strategic partnerships with other energy-producing nations.

5. Socio-Economic Impact:

a. Employment and Workforce Transitions: We will discuss the potential socio-economic impact of the changing energy landscape on oil-dependent economies, including the need for workforce transitions, retraining programs, and the creation of new job opportunities in emerging sectors.

b. Social and Economic Development: We will explore how the shift towards renewable energy can contribute to social and economic development, including the potential for decentralized energy systems, rural electrification, and the promotion of sustainable development goals.

Conclusion:

The changing energy landscape presents both challenges and opportunities for oil-rich countries in the Middle East. Adapting to these changes requires proactive strategies that promote economic diversification, technological innovation, environmental sustainability, and geopolitical flexibility. By embracing the transition to renewable energy, investing in energy efficiency measures, and considering the socio-economic implications, oil-rich countries can navigate the changing energy landscape and secure a sustainable and prosperous future.

Chapter 7: Future Perspectives and Emerging Trends

Youth Demographics and Political Activism

The youth population plays a crucial role in shaping the future of African and Middle Eastern politics. This section examines the significance of youth demographics and explores the dynamics of political activism among young people. It delves into the motivations, challenges, and potential impact of youth engagement in the political sphere.

1. Youth Demographics and Socioeconomic Context:

a. Youth Population Growth: We will explore the demographic trends in African and Middle Eastern countries, highlighting the significant youth bulge and its implications for political dynamics. This includes an analysis of population structures, urbanization, and the impact of youth unemployment.

b. Socioeconomic Challenges: We will discuss the socio-economic challenges faced by young people, such as limited access to education, unemployment, poverty, and inequality. We will examine how these factors influence their political attitudes and aspirations.

2. Motivations for Political Activism:

a. Desire for Change and Reform: We will explore the motivations driving young people to engage in political activism, including their aspirations for social justice, political freedom, and economic opportunities. We will discuss how these motivations are influenced by historical, cultural, and socio-economic factors.

b. Technological Advancements and Digital Activism: We will examine the role of technology, social media, and digital platforms in facilitating political mobilization among young people. We will discuss the impact of online activism, digital campaigns, and the use of social media as tools for organizing and expressing political demands.

3. Forms of Youth Political Activism:

a. Street Protests and Demonstrations: We will analyze the prevalence of street protests and mass demonstrations as a form of youth political activism. We will explore the factors that lead young people to take to the streets, the tactics employed, and the outcomes and challenges associated with these movements.

b. Youth-led Organizations and Movements: We will examine the emergence of youth-led organizations and movements that focus on political and social issues. We will explore their strategies, goals, and the impact they have on policy debates, advocacy efforts, and grassroots mobilization.

c. Youth Political Participation: We will discuss the extent of youth political participation, including their engagement in formal political processes, such as voting, running for office, and joining political parties. We will also explore the barriers and opportunities young people face in participating in decision-making structures.

4. Challenges and Opportunities:

a. Repression and State Responses: We will analyze the challenges faced by young activists, including state repression, surveillance, and the suppression of dissent. We will discuss the strategies employed by governments to control youth movements and the implications for political dynamics.

b. Collaboration with Established Political Actors: We will examine the potential for collaboration and alliances between youth activists and established political actors, such as political parties, civil society organizations, and international institutions. We will discuss the benefits, tensions, and challenges associated with such collaborations.

c. Capacity Building and Empowerment: We will explore the importance of capacity building initiatives and youth empowerment programs in nurturing effective and sustainable political activism. We will discuss the role of education, leadership development, and mentorship in empowering young people to become agents of change.

5. Impact and Future Prospects:

a. Influence on Policy and Decision Making: We will assess the impact of youth political activism on policy agendas, decision-making processes, and governance structures. We will explore case studies and examples where youth movements have successfully influenced political outcomes and initiated policy reforms.

b. Long-term Implications: We will discuss the long-term implications of youth political activism, including its potential to shape the future of African and Middle Eastern politics. We will examine the prospects for sustainable political engagement, the transition from activism to leadership, and the potential for intergenerational collaboration.

Conclusion:

Youth demographics and political activism are key drivers of change and transformation in African and Middle Eastern politics. This section highlights the significance of the youth population, explores their motivations for political engagement, and examines the various forms of youth activism. It also addresses the challenges faced by young activists and explores the opportunities for collaboration and empowerment. By understanding the dynamics of youth political activism, we can gain insights into the future prospects and potentials for political change in these regions.

Technological Advancements and Digital Transformation

Technological advancements and digital transformation have had a profound impact on African and Middle Eastern politics, shaping the way information is accessed, shared, and mobilized. This section explores the role of technology in political landscapes, examining the opportunities and challenges it presents for governance, activism, and public discourse.

1. Digital Connectivity and Access:

a. Internet Penetration: We will discuss the progress of internet connectivity in African and Middle Eastern countries, analyzing the factors influencing the digital divide and the implications for political participation and access to information.

b. Mobile Phone Revolution: We will examine the widespread adoption of mobile phones and their impact on political communication, social mobilization, and citizen engagement. We will explore case studies of successful mobile-based initiatives and their role in driving political change.

2. Social Media and Political Mobilization:

a. Rise of Social Media Platforms: We will explore the proliferation of social media platforms in the region and their significance as tools for political mobilization, organizing protests, and disseminating information. We will discuss the impact of platforms such as Facebook, Twitter, and WhatsApp on political discourse and activism.

b. Online Activism and Hashtag Campaigns: We will examine the emergence of online activism and hashtag campaigns as powerful tools for raising awareness, mobilizing support, and amplifying marginalized voices. We will discuss the successes and challenges of digital activism in bringing about political change.

3. Fake News, Disinformation, and Digital Manipulation:

a. Spread of Misinformation: We will address the challenges posed by the spread of fake news, disinformation, and online manipulation in the context of African and Middle Eastern politics. We will discuss the impact of these phenomena on public opinion, electoral processes, and trust in institutions.

b. Role of State Actors and Non-State Actors: We will examine the role of state actors, political parties, and non-state actors in leveraging digital platforms for propaganda, cyber warfare, and influencing public discourse. We will discuss strategies to counter disinformation and promote media literacy.

4. E-Governance and Citizen Engagement:

a. Digital Government Services: We will explore the advancements in e-governance and the digitization of public services in African and Middle Eastern countries. We will discuss the potential of digital platforms for improving government transparency, efficiency, and citizen engagement.

b. Online Platforms for Public Participation: We will examine the use of online platforms for public consultation, participatory budgeting, and policy-making. We will discuss the opportunities and challenges of digital tools in fostering inclusive and responsive governance.

5. Data Privacy and Digital Rights:

a. Data Protection and Privacy Laws: We will discuss the importance of data protection and privacy laws in the digital age, analyzing the regulatory frameworks in African and Middle Eastern countries. We will explore the challenges of balancing national security concerns with individual rights.

b. Digital Surveillance and Freedom of Expression: We will address the implications of digital surveillance, censorship, and restrictions on freedom of expression in the region. We will examine the efforts to protect digital rights, promote online privacy, and ensure internet freedom.

6. Technological Innovations and Emerging Trends:

a. Artificial Intelligence and Big Data: We will explore the potential of artificial intelligence and big data analytics in shaping political landscapes, including their use in election campaigns, policy formulation, and governance. We will discuss the ethical and social implications of these technologies.

b. Blockchain Technology and Decentralization: We will examine the applications of blockchain technology in enhancing transparency, accountability, and trust in governance systems. We will discuss the potential of blockchain for secure voting systems, digital identities, and anti-corruption efforts.

Conclusion:

Technological advancements and digital transformation have the power to reshape African and Middle Eastern politics, fostering new forms of political participation, amplifying marginalized voices, and challenging existing power structures. However, they also bring about new challenges such as fake news, data privacy concerns, and digital inequalities. By understanding the impact of technology on political dynamics, policymakers, activists, and citizens can harness its potential for positive change while addressing the associated risks and limitations.

Climate Change and Environmental Pressures

Climate change and environmental issues have become critical factors shaping the future of African and Middle Eastern politics. This section explores the impact of climate change on the regions, analyzes the environmental challenges they face, and examines the political responses to mitigate and adapt to these pressures. It also discusses the implications of climate change for social stability, resource management, and regional cooperation.

1. Climate Change and its Impacts:

a. Climate Change Science: We will provide an overview of the scientific consensus on climate change, emphasizing the specific impacts on African and Middle Eastern countries. We will discuss rising temperatures, changing rainfall patterns, sea-level rise, and the consequences for ecosystems, agriculture, and water resources.

b. Environmental Vulnerabilities: We will examine the vulnerabilities of the regions to climate change, including their dependence on rain-fed agriculture, exposure to natural disasters, and limited adaptive capacity. We will explore the disproportionate impact on marginalized communities and vulnerable groups.

2. Water Scarcity and Resource Management:

a. Water Stress and Security: We will discuss the growing challenges of water scarcity and the potential for water-related conflicts in African and Middle Eastern countries. We will examine the competition for water resources, transboundary water issues, and the need for sustainable water management practices.

b. Renewable Energy and Water Desalination: We will explore the role of renewable energy in addressing the energy-water nexus, emphasizing the potential of solar and wind power. We will also discuss the importance of water desalination technologies in ensuring water security in water-scarce regions.

3. Food Security and Agricultural Adaptation:

a. Agricultural Challenges: We will analyze the impact of climate change on agricultural productivity, food security, and rural livelihoods in African and Middle Eastern countries. We will discuss the need for adaptive farming practices, resilient crop varieties, and sustainable land management techniques.

b. Innovation and Technology: We will explore innovative approaches to agricultural adaptation, such as climate-smart agriculture, precision farming, and agroecology. We will discuss the role of technology transfer, capacity building, and international cooperation in supporting agricultural resilience.

4. Environmental Degradation and Ecosystem Conservation:

a. Deforestation and Biodiversity Loss: We will examine the drivers of deforestation, habitat degradation, and biodiversity loss in the regions. We will discuss the impacts on ecosystems, wildlife, and the services they provide, emphasizing the need for conservation strategies and protected areas.

b. Sustainable Resource Management: We will explore the importance of sustainable resource management practices, including responsible forestry, fisheries management, and protected area networks. We will discuss the role of community-based approaches, indigenous knowledge, and public-private partnerships.

5. Climate Change and Social Stability:

a. Climate-induced Migration and Displacement: We will analyze the links between climate change, migration, and displacement in African and Middle Eastern contexts. We will discuss the challenges faced by climate refugees, the potential for conflict over scarce resources, and the need for international cooperation in addressing these issues.

b. Social and Political Resilience: We will examine the role of social resilience, adaptive governance, and community-based approaches in building resilience to climate change. We will discuss the importance of integrating climate change considerations into development policies and strategies.

6. Regional Cooperation and International Commitments:

a. Regional Environmental Agreements: We will examine existing regional environmental agreements and initiatives in Africa and the Middle East, such as the African Union's Agenda 2063 and the Arab League's Environmental Strategy. We will discuss the challenges and opportunities for regional cooperation in addressing climate change and environmental issues.

b. Global Climate Diplomacy: We will explore the role of African and Middle Eastern countries in global climate negotiations, including their commitments under the United Nations Framework Convention on Climate Change (UNFCCC) and the Paris Agreement. We will discuss the importance of international cooperation, climate finance, and technology transfer in supporting climate action.

Conclusion:

The chapter concludes by emphasizing the urgent need for proactive and coordinated action to address climate change and environmental pressures in African and Middle Eastern countries. It highlights the potential for innovative solutions, collaborative governance, and inclusive approaches to build resilience and ensure a sustainable future for the regions. By prioritizing climate action and integrating environmental considerations into policymaking, the countries can navigate the complex challenges and seize the opportunities presented by a changing climate.

Potential Scenarios and Prospects for African and Middle Eastern Politics

This section delves into potential scenarios and prospects for African and Middle Eastern politics, considering the evolving dynamics and emerging trends in the regions. It explores various future trajectories, challenges, and opportunities that could shape political landscapes. By examining different scenarios, this section aims to provide insights into the potential outcomes and the factors that could influence the future direction of African and Middle Eastern politics.

Scenario 1: Democratic Consolidation and Economic Progress:

a. Political Reforms and Institutional Strengthening: We will explore the potential for further democratic consolidation in the regions, analyzing the role of robust institutions, electoral reforms, and inclusive governance. We will discuss the importance of accountable leadership, transparency, and the rule of law in promoting political stability and economic progress.

b. Economic Diversification and Sustainable Development: We will examine the prospects for economic diversification beyond resource dependence, focusing on sectors such as technology, renewable energy, and manufacturing. We will discuss the potential for job creation, entrepreneurship, and sustainable development as catalysts for political stability and social cohesion.

Scenario 2: Socio-Political Transformation and Social Movements:

a. Youth Mobilization and Activism: We will explore the role of youth demographics in driving socio-political transformation, emphasizing the power of youth mobilization, social movements, and demands for change. We will discuss the potential for youth-led initiatives, civic engagement, and grassroots activism to shape the political landscape.

b. Gender Equality and Women's Empowerment: We will examine the prospects for gender equality and women's empowerment in African and Middle Eastern politics. We will discuss the potential for increased political representation, access to education and healthcare, and the dismantling of gender-based barriers as transformative factors.

Scenario 3: Regional Cooperation and Integration:

a. Economic Integration and Trade Cooperation: We will analyze the potential for enhanced regional economic integration, trade cooperation, and infrastructure development. We will discuss the prospects for regional trade blocs, such as the African Continental Free Trade Area (AfCFTA), and the impact of increased economic integration on political dynamics.

b. Security Cooperation and Conflict Resolution: We will explore the potential for strengthened security cooperation and conflict resolution mechanisms in the regions. We will discuss the prospects for regional organizations, such as the African Union and the Arab League, in addressing security challenges and promoting stability.

Scenario 4: Environmental Sustainability and Climate Action:

a. Climate Change Mitigation and Adaptation: We will examine the prospects for increased environmental awareness, climate change mitigation efforts, and adaptation strategies. We will discuss the potential for renewable energy development, sustainable agriculture practices, and conservation initiatives to shape political priorities and foster regional cooperation.

b. Water and Resource Management: We will explore the potential for collaborative water management, resource sharing, and sustainable use of natural resources. We will discuss the prospects for transboundary agreements, ecosystem restoration, and sustainable resource governance as drivers of political cooperation and stability.

Conclusion:

The chapter concludes by emphasizing that the future of African and Middle Eastern politics will depend on a multitude of factors and interactions between various scenarios. It highlights the importance of proactive and visionary leadership, inclusive governance, and regional cooperation in shaping positive outcomes. By considering potential scenarios and understanding the opportunities and challenges they present, the regions can navigate their political landscapes and strive towards a future characterized by stability, prosperity, and social progress.

Conclusion

Recap of Key Insights on African and Middle Eastern Politics

The conclusion of the book "Political Landscapes: African Politics and Middle Eastern Dynamics" offers a comprehensive recap of the key insights gained throughout the chapters, providing a synthesized overview of the complexities and nuances of African and Middle Eastern politics. By revisiting the main themes, challenges, and opportunities discussed in the preceding chapters, this section aims to consolidate the understanding of the political landscapes in these regions and highlight their significance in the global context.

1. Historical Context and Colonial Legacies:

a. The Legacy of Colonialism: This section revisits the historical context and colonial legacies that have shaped African and Middle Eastern politics. It highlights the impact of European colonization, the partitioning of territories, and the lingering effects of colonial rule on political systems, borders, and identity formation.

b. Nationalism and Independence Movements: The role of nationalism and independence movements in reshaping the political landscape is discussed. The emergence of post-colonial states, their struggles for self-determination, and the challenges they faced in nation-building are analyzed.

2. Economic, Social, and Cultural Diversity in the Regions:

a. Economic Diversity: This section revisits the economic diversity within African and Middle Eastern countries, highlighting the presence of resource-rich nations, agricultural economies, and emerging industries. The significance of economic disparities, poverty, and inequality in shaping political dynamics is discussed.

b. Social and Cultural Factors: The diversity of social and cultural factors within the regions is revisited, emphasizing the role of religion, ethnicity, tribalism, and linguistic diversity in shaping political identities, power dynamics, and social cohesion.

3. African Political Landscapes:

a. Post-Colonialism and Nation-Building Challenges: This section recapitulates the challenges faced by African nations in the post-colonial era, including state-building, governance issues, and the complexities of ethnic politics.

b. Ethnic Politics and Identity-Based Conflicts: The influence of ethnic politics and identity-based conflicts on African political landscapes is revisited. The impact of ethnic divisions, struggles for power, and the role of political parties in managing diversity are explored.

c. Corruption and Governance Issues: The persistence of corruption and governance challenges in African politics is reiterated. The detrimental effects of corruption on development, accountability, and political stability are discussed.

d. Economic Development and Foreign Aid Dependency: The interplay between economic development and foreign aid dependency is revisited, emphasizing the importance of sustainable economic growth, investment in human capital, and reducing reliance on external assistance.

4. African Democratic Transitions:

a. Democratization Waves and Political Reforms: This section recapitulates the waves of democratization that have swept across African nations, highlighting the importance of political reforms, electoral processes, and the consolidation of democratic institutions.

b. Challenges of Building Strong Institutions: The challenges faced in building strong institutions and the significance of independent judiciaries, free media, and civil society in sustaining democratic transitions are revisited.

c. Role of Civil Society in Democratization: The role of civil society organizations, grassroots movements, and citizen participation in fostering democratic governance and holding political leaders accountable is emphasized.

d. Case Studies of Successful Democratic Transitions: This section revisits case studies of successful democratic transitions in African countries, such as South Africa and Ghana. The factors contributing to their success, including leadership, societal resilience, and regional support, are discussed.

5. Middle Eastern Political Dynamics:

a. Historical and Geopolitical Factors Shaping the Region: The historical and geopolitical factors that have shaped the Middle Eastern region, including colonial interventions, power struggles, and the Israeli-Palestinian conflict, are revisited.

b. Sunni-Shia Divide and Sectarianism: The sectarian tensions and the Sunni-Shia divide that have influenced political dynamics in the Middle East are discussed. The impact of sectarian conflicts on regional stability, state-society relations, and proxy wars is emphasized.

c. Arab Spring and Its Aftermath: The Arab Spring and its consequences for Middle Eastern politics are recapitulated. The popular uprisings, demands for political reforms, and the subsequent challenges and setbacks are analyzed.

d. Role of Non-State Actors in the Middle East: The role of non-state actors, including militant groups, terrorist organizations, and transnational movements, in shaping Middle Eastern politics is revisited. The impact of non-state actors on state sovereignty, security dynamics, and regional power struggles is discussed.

6. Israeli-Palestinian Conflict:

a. Historical Background and Key Events: The historical background of the Israeli-Palestinian conflict and the key events that have shaped its trajectory, such as the Balfour Declaration, the establishment of Israel, and the various peace processes, are recapitulated.

b. Territorial Disputes and Settlements: The territorial disputes, including the status of Jerusalem, the West Bank, and Gaza Strip, and the impact of Israeli settlements on the peace process, are revisited. The challenges and complexities of finding a mutually acceptable solution are discussed.

c. Peace Process and Two-State Solution: The peace process and the pursuit of a two-state solution as a framework for resolving the Israeli-Palestinian conflict are emphasized. The obstacles, such as security concerns, political divisions, and the role of external actors, are revisited.

d. International Perspectives and Mediation Efforts: The role of international actors, including the United States, the United Nations, and regional organizations, in mediating the Israeli-Palestinian conflict is discussed. The prospects for international initiatives and the impact of changing geopolitical dynamics on the peace process are explored.

7. Regional Rivalries in the Middle East:

a. Iran-Saudi Arabia Power Struggle: The power struggle between Iran and Saudi Arabia and its implications for regional stability and security are recapitulated. The religious, political, and ideological dimensions of the rivalry, as well as their regional proxy conflicts, are discussed.

b. Proxy Conflicts and Sectarian Tensions: The prevalence of proxy conflicts and sectarian tensions in the Middle East is revisited. The impact of these conflicts on regional dynamics, state sovereignty, and the involvement of external powers is analyzed.

c. Role of External Powers in Regional Dynamics: The role of external powers, such as the United States, Russia, and major global players, in shaping Middle Eastern politics is emphasized. The influence of external actors on regional alliances, arms sales, and power dynamics is discussed.

d. Impact of Regional Rivalries on Stability and Security: The implications of regional rivalries on stability and security in the Middle East are revisited. The risks of escalation, the impact on humanitarian crises, and the challenges of conflict resolution are discussed.

8. Oil Politics and Resource Curse:

a. Importance of Oil in Middle Eastern Politics: The significance of oil in Middle Eastern politics is recapitulated. The role of oil in shaping economies, political alliances, and regional power dynamics is discussed.

b. Resource Curse Phenomenon and Economic Challenges: The resource curse phenomenon and its impact on economic development, governance, and social inequality are revisited. The challenges of managing oil wealth, diversifying economies, and mitigating the adverse effects of resource dependence are discussed.

c. Diversification and Sustainable Development: The prospects for economic diversification and sustainable development in the context of oil-rich Middle Eastern countries are emphasized. The importance of investing in human capital, fostering innovation, and transitioning towards renewable energy sources is discussed.

d. Implications of Changing Energy Landscape: The implications of the changing energy landscape, including the rise of renewable energy and global efforts to combat climate change, are discussed. The opportunities and challenges for

Middle Eastern countries in adapting to these shifts are revisited.

9. Future Perspectives and Emerging Trends:

a. Youth Demographics and Political Activism: The demographic significance of youth populations in Africa and the Middle East and their role in shaping political activism, social movements, and demands for change are emphasized. The potential for generational shifts in political landscapes is discussed.

b. Technological Advancements and Digital Transformation: The impact of technological advancements and the digital transformation on political participation, information dissemination, and governance in Africa and the Middle East are revisited. The challenges and opportunities presented by digital platforms and social media are discussed.

c. Climate Change and Environmental Pressures: The implications of climate change and environmental pressures for political stability, resource management, and human security in Africa and the Middle East are discussed. The need for regional cooperation and sustainable environmental policies is emphasized.

d. Potential Scenarios and Prospects for African and Middle Eastern Politics: This section provides a synthesis of potential future scenarios and prospects for African and Middle Eastern politics. It explores various possibilities, including political reforms, regional integration, economic diversification, and geopolitical realignments.

Conclusion:

The conclusion summarizes the key insights gained from the book and emphasizes the importance of understanding the complexities of African and Middle Eastern politics. It highlights the interconnectedness of regional dynamics, the significance of historical legacies, and the role of internal and external actors in shaping political landscapes. The conclusion also acknowledges the challenges and opportunities that lie ahead, emphasizing the need for inclusive governance, sustainable development, and regional cooperation in order to address the pressing issues and ensure a more stable and prosperous future for the regions.

Challenges and Opportunities for the Regions

Introduction: The conclusion of this book on African and Middle Eastern politics provides an opportunity to reflect on the challenges and opportunities that lie ahead for these regions. Over the course of the chapters, we have explored the historical, political, social, and economic dynamics that shape the African and Middle Eastern landscapes. In this final section, we will synthesize the key challenges faced by the regions and the potential opportunities that can be harnessed to overcome these challenges and foster positive change.

1. Socioeconomic Challenges: a. Poverty and Inequality: Africa and the Middle East continue to grapple with high levels of poverty and income inequality. The challenge of addressing poverty and promoting inclusive growth requires concerted efforts from governments, civil society, and the international community.

b. Youth Unemployment: The high rates of youth unemployment in both regions present a significant challenge. Creating employment opportunities, improving education and skills training, and promoting entrepreneurship are crucial for harnessing the demographic dividend and ensuring a prosperous future.

c.   Economic   Diversification: Overreliance   on extractive industries, such as oil in the Middle East, poses risks to long-term economic stability. Diversifying the economies, investing in sectors such as agriculture, manufacturing, and technology, and promoting innovation and entrepreneurship can mitigate vulnerabilities and create sustainable growth.

2.   Governance   and   Political   Challenges: a. Democratization and Governance Reforms: Consolidating democratic transitions, strengthening institutions, and promoting accountable and transparent governance remain pressing challenges. Upholding the rule of law, protecting human rights, and combating corruption are vital for fostering political stability and citizen trust.

b. Ethnic and Identity-Based Conflicts: Ethnic and identity-based conflicts persist in both regions, undermining social cohesion and political stability. Encouraging dialogue, promoting social inclusion, and addressing historical grievances are necessary for fostering peaceful coexistence and inclusive societies.

c. Security and Terrorism: Africa and the Middle East continue to face security challenges, including terrorism, insurgency, and transnational crime. Cooperation among regional and international actors, intelligence sharing, and addressing the root causes of extremism are crucial for maintaining stability and security.

3. Regional Cooperation and Integration: a. Economic Integration: Enhancing regional economic integration can unlock significant opportunities for trade, investment, and economic development. Strengthening regional organizations, harmonizing policies, and removing trade barriers can foster economic cooperation and promote shared prosperity.

b. Peace and Security Cooperation: Addressing regional conflicts and promoting peaceful resolutions require enhanced cooperation among countries and regional organizations. Collaborative efforts in conflict prevention, peacekeeping, and post-conflict reconstruction can contribute to regional stability.

c. Water and Resource Management: Managing shared resources, such as water, is essential for preventing conflicts and promoting sustainable development. Regional frameworks for cooperation, dialogue, and joint management of resources can mitigate tensions and foster cooperation.

4. Harnessing Technology and Innovation: a. Digital Transformation: Embracing the digital revolution can bring numerous benefits to African and Middle Eastern societies.

Expanding access to technology, investing in digital infrastructure, and promoting digital literacy can enhance governance, service delivery, and economic opportunities.

b. Innovation and Entrepreneurship: Fostering innovation and entrepreneurship can spur economic growth, create jobs, and drive sustainable development. Supporting startups, providing access to finance, and creating an enabling environment for innovation can unlock the creative potential of the regions.

5. Environmental Sustainability: a. Climate Change Mitigation and Adaptation: The impact of climate change on Africa and the Middle East is significant and poses a threat to ecosystems, agriculture, and human security. Implementing climate change mitigation measures, promoting renewable energy, and investing in adaptive strategies are essential for long-term sustainability.

b. Sustainable Natural Resource Management: Ensuring sustainable management of natural resources, including water, forests, and biodiversity, is crucial for preserving ecosystems and supporting livelihoods. Adopting sustainable practices, investing in conservation, and promoting responsible resource extraction can contribute to environmental sustainability.

Conclusion: The challenges faced by Africa and the Middle East are significant, but they also present opportunities for positive change and transformation. By addressing socioeconomic disparities, strengthening governance, fostering regional cooperation, harnessing technological advancements, and prioritizing environmental sustainability, the regions can overcome these challenges and realize their full potential. It is through collaborative efforts, inclusive governance, and a commitment to sustainable development that Africa and the Middle East can shape a prosperous and stable future for their citizens and contribute to global peace and prosperity.

Importance of Regional Cooperation and Global Engagement

Introduction: In this concluding chapter, we will discuss the importance of regional cooperation and global engagement in the context of African and Middle Eastern politics. Throughout this book, we have explored the historical, political, and social dynamics of these regions and examined the challenges and opportunities they face. In this section, we will emphasize the significance of regional cooperation and engagement with the international community as essential drivers of progress, stability, and development.

1. Regional Cooperation: a. Economic Integration: Regional economic integration holds immense potential for African and Middle Eastern countries. By fostering closer economic ties, eliminating trade barriers, and harmonizing policies, countries can create larger markets, attract foreign investment, and boost economic growth. Examples such as the African Continental Free Trade Area (AfCFTA) and the Gulf Cooperation Council (GCC) demonstrate the benefits of regional economic cooperation.

b. Peace and Security: Regional cooperation is critical for addressing conflicts and maintaining peace and security. By sharing intelligence, coordinating military efforts, and promoting dialogue, countries can effectively combat terrorism, transnational crime, and destabilizing activities. Regional organizations like the African Union (AU) and the League of Arab States play crucial roles in conflict resolution and peacekeeping.

c. Resource Management: Managing shared resources, such as water and energy, requires regional cooperation. By establishing frameworks for equitable resource allocation, joint management, and dispute resolution, countries can prevent conflicts and ensure sustainable use of resources. The Nile Basin Initiative and the Red Sea-Dead Sea Conduit project are examples of regional initiatives in resource management.

2. Diplomacy and Global Engagement: a. Strengthening Diplomatic Relations: Robust diplomatic ties between African and Middle Eastern countries and the rest of the world are essential for political, economic, and cultural exchange. Engaging in diplomatic dialogues, fostering diplomatic missions, and participating in international organizations enable countries to address global challenges, promote their interests, and build mutually beneficial partnerships.

b. Economic Partnerships: Engaging with the global economy through trade, investment, and technology transfer is vital for economic growth. African and Middle Eastern countries can attract foreign direct investment, access new markets, and benefit from knowledge and technology transfers through strategic partnerships with global actors. Building strong economic relationships can promote inclusive growth and enhance competitiveness.

c. Addressing Global Challenges: African and Middle Eastern countries face a range of global challenges, including climate change, terrorism, and migration. These issues require collective action and global cooperation. By engaging in multilateral forums, participating in global initiatives, and adhering to international agreements, countries can contribute to finding collective solutions to global challenges.

3. Cultural Exchange and Soft Power: a. Cultural Diplomacy: Cultural exchange and understanding are essential for fostering peace, promoting dialogue, and building bridges between nations. African and Middle Eastern countries possess rich cultural heritage, and by promoting cultural diplomacy, they can enhance their soft power, boost tourism, and foster people-to-people connections.

b. Education and Knowledge Exchange: Collaboration in education and knowledge exchange facilitates human capital development and the sharing of best practices. By promoting student exchanges, scholarships, and academic partnerships, countries can invest in their human resources and benefit from diverse perspectives and expertise.

c. Media and Public Diplomacy: Utilizing media platforms effectively can shape public opinion, challenge misconceptions, and project positive narratives. African and Middle Eastern countries can enhance their global image and promote their achievements, culture, and values through strategic public diplomacy and media engagement.

4. Humanitarian Assistance and Development Cooperation: a. Humanitarian Aid: Both African and Middle Eastern regions face humanitarian crises, including conflicts, displacement, and natural disasters. International humanitarian assistance plays a crucial role in alleviating suffering, providing essential services, and rebuilding communities. Engaging with the international community enables countries to access resources, expertise, and support in times of crisis.

b. Development Cooperation: Collaborating with international development agencies and partners is crucial for addressing development challenges. Through development cooperation, countries can access funding, technical assistance, and capacity-building programs to support infrastructure development, poverty reduction, and social welfare initiatives.

Conclusion

Regional cooperation and global engagement are paramount for the progress, stability, and development of African and Middle Eastern countries. By fostering regional economic integration, promoting peace and security, managing shared resources, and engaging with the global community, these regions can overcome challenges, harness opportunities, and achieve sustainable development. Building strong diplomatic relations, addressing global challenges, promoting cultural exchange, and engaging in humanitarian and development cooperation are integral to shaping a prosperous and interconnected future for Africa, the Middle East, and the world.

THE END

Key Terms and Definitions

To help you better understand the language and concepts related to aging and older adults, below you will find a list of key terms and their definitions.

Key Terms

1. Regional Cooperation: The process of collaboration and mutual assistance among countries within a specific geographic region to address common challenges, promote economic integration, enhance security, and foster political dialogue.

2. Global Engagement: Active participation and involvement of countries in international affairs, including diplomatic relations, economic partnerships, and cooperation in addressing global issues.

3. Economic Integration: The process of reducing trade barriers, harmonizing economic policies, and facilitating the flow of goods, services, and capital among countries within a specific region to promote economic growth, enhance competitiveness, and create larger markets.

4. Peace and Security: The state of freedom from conflict, violence, and the threat of aggression. Peace and security are fundamental prerequisites for stability, development, and the well-being of societies.

5. Resource Management: The sustainable and equitable utilization, allocation, and preservation of shared resources, such as water, energy, and natural resources, to avoid conflicts, promote cooperation, and ensure long-term environmental sustainability.

6. Diplomacy: The practice of conducting negotiations, maintaining relations, and representing the interests of a country or organization through dialogue, negotiation, and peaceful means. Diplomacy plays a crucial role in building relationships, resolving disputes, and promoting cooperation.

7. Soft Power: The ability of a country or entity to influence others through attraction, persuasion, and cultural values rather than through military or economic coercion. Soft power includes elements such as cultural diplomacy, education, and the projection of positive image and values.

8. Humanitarian Assistance: The provision of aid, support, and resources to alleviate suffering and meet the immediate needs of people affected by crises, such as conflicts, natural disasters, or humanitarian emergencies.

9. Development Cooperation: Collaboration between countries, international organizations, and development agencies to promote sustainable development, reduce

poverty, and address socio-economic challenges through the transfer of knowledge, resources, and technical assistance.

10. Global Challenges: Complex issues that transcend national boundaries and require collective action and cooperation among countries to find effective solutions. Examples include climate change, terrorism, migration, and global health pandemics.

11. Cultural Diplomacy: The use of cultural exchanges, arts, language, and cultural events to build understanding, promote dialogue, and enhance relations between countries, fostering mutual respect and appreciation of diverse cultures.

12. Sustainable Development: Development that meets the needs of the present generation without compromising the ability of future generations to meet their own needs. Sustainable development balances economic growth, social well-being, and environmental protection.

Supporting Materials

Introduction:

Huntington, Samuel P. "The Third Wave: Democratization in the Late Twentieth Century." University of Oklahoma Press, 1991.

Goldstone, Jack A. "Revolutions: A Very Short Introduction." Oxford University Press, 2014.

Halliday, Fred. "The Middle East in International Relations: Power, Politics and Ideology." Cambridge University Press, 2018.

Chapter 1: African Political Landscapes:

Acemoglu, Daron, and James A. Robinson. "Why Nations Fail: The Origins of Power, Prosperity, and Poverty." Crown Business, 2012.

Mamdani, Mahmood. "Citizen and Subject: Contemporary Africa and the Legacy of Late Colonialism." Princeton University Press, 1996.

Chabal, Patrick, and Jean-Pascal Daloz. "Africa Works: Disorder as Political Instrument." Oxford University Press, 1999.

Chapter 2: African Democratic Transitions:

Bratton, Michael, and Nicolas Van de Walle. "Democratic Experiments in Africa: Regime Transitions in Comparative Perspective." Cambridge University Press, 1997.

Cheeseman, Nic, and Brian Klaas. "How to Rig an Election." Yale University Press, 2018.

Lindberg, Staffan I. "Democratization by Elections: A New Mode of Transition." Johns Hopkins University Press, 2009.

Chapter 3: Middle Eastern Political Dynamics:

Fawcett, Louise. "International Relations of the Middle East." Oxford University Press, 2019.

Heydemann, Steven, and Reinoud Leenders. "Middle East Authoritarianisms: Governance, Contestation, and Regime Resilience in Syria and Iran." Stanford University Press, 2013.

Beinin, Joel, and Frederic Vairel. "Social Movements, Mobilization, and Contestation in the Middle East and North Africa." Stanford University Press, 2013.

Chapter 4: Israeli-Palestinian Conflict:

Morris, Benny. "Righteous Victims: A History of the Zionist-Arab Conflict, 1881-2001." Vintage, 2001.

Shlaim, Avi. "The Iron Wall: Israel and the Arab World." W. W. Norton & Company, 2014.

Khalidi, Rashid. "The Iron Cage: The Story of the Palestinian Struggle for Statehood." Beacon Press, 2007.

Chapter 5: Regional Rivalries in the Middle East:

Lynch, Marc. "The New Arab Wars: Uprisings and Anarchy in the Middle East." PublicAffairs, 2016.

Gause III, F. Gregory. "Beyond Sectarianism: The New Middle East Cold War." Brookings Institution Press, 2014.

Nasr, Vali. "The Shia Revival: How Conflicts within Islam Will Shape the Future." W. W. Norton & Company, 2006.

Chapter 6: Oil Politics and Resource Curse:

Ross, Michael L. "The Oil Curse: How Petroleum Wealth Shapes the Development of Nations." Princeton University Press, 2012.

Karl, Terry Lynn. "The Paradox of Plenty: Oil Booms and Petro-States." University of California Press, 1997.

Klare, Michael T. "Resource Wars: The New Landscape of Global Conflict." Henry Holt and Company, 2002.

Chapter 7: Future Perspectives and Emerging Trends:

Moeller, Susan D. "The Digital Pueblo: Technological Futures and Indigenous Peoples." University of Texas Press, 2005.

Slaughter, Anne-Marie. "The Chessboard and the Web: Strategies of Connection in a Networked World." Yale University Press, 2017.

Steffen, Will, et al. "The Anthropocene: From Global Change to Planetary Stewardship." Annual Review of Environment and Resources, 2015.

Conclusion:

Lijphart, Arend. "Democracies: Patterns of Majoritarian and Consensus Government in Twenty-One Countries." Yale University Press, 2012.

Nye Jr., Joseph S. "Soft Power: The Means to Success in World Politics." PublicAffairs, 2004.

Fukuyama, Francis. "The End of History and the Last Man." Free Press, 1992.

www.ingramcontent.com/pod-product-compliance
Lightning Source LLC
Chambersburg PA
CBHW060043030426
42334CB00019B/2462